D0181735

"Steve walks beside us telling us stories, drawing images, cracking jokes and pointing out the evidence that human intelligence can deliver so much more than we allow it … a welcome guide to the learning journey."

Marilyn Hamilton, Ph.D., C.G.A., Founder of Integral City

"Weaving Collaborative Intelligence (CQ) into organizations is an idea for it's time. Instilling CQ in the learning and actions of all employees of an organization is a vital resource to engage everyone in the real work. Joyce's book is a must read."

Dr. Stephen Hobbs, author *Help Them to Help YOU Lead*

"Stephen delights in bringing us to a richer realization, and more complete picture of our collaborative intelligence. A practical book that points out the skills that enable us to master our own collaborative capacity."

J. Brian Woodward, Ph.D. Senior Faculty,
Leadership Development & Leadership Learning Lab,
The Banff Centre, Canada

"Get out of autopilot and read this book. Full of wisdom and insight, you may not think about work and the difference you can make, in quite the same way ever again…"

Paul Belcher, Trainer, Consultant and Coach, ABL World

"Stephen has the uncanny ability to make the complex understood. *Teaching an Anthill to Fetch* is about liberating human potential. Insightful as it is practical, the author puts forward a simple set of higher order rules that organizations can use to succeed, regardless of what the future might bring. …rediscover the unbounded resilience that lies at our fingertips when we come together and collaborate effectively."

Clifford Wessel, Performance Consultant & Coach

"Immediately useful…. *Teaching an Anthill to Fetch* is a contemplative practice for building a better life."

Don Hill, Media Thought Leader

"Anyone who enjoys a good story will certainly relish the Irish lilt of Joyce's voice which comes through on each and every page."

Michael K. Mauws, Ph.D., Associate Professor, Business Policy & Strategy, Athabasca University

"*Teaching an Anthill to Fetch* provides a valuable path to strengthen the emergent survival skill — collaboration. With novel features like "Go Deeper" and practical "Tools", this is a new road map to make *Collaborative Intelligence* really work @ *Work*!"

Roger Gullickson, President/CEO, MVP Collaborative

"*Teaching an Anthill to Fetch* is a must-read. This book provides valuable insights that will benefit any organization undertaking change and wanting to get the most out of its most important asset — its human resources."

Rick Thrale, Community Futures, Alberta

"[*Teaching an Anthill to Fetch* is] … a practical handbook with suggestions and exercises to help us to improve our team's "Collaborative Intelligence". A great addition to the canon of leadership literature."

Peter McNab, author of *Towards An Integral Vision*

"This book will help managers and team leaders see the learning terrain more clearly … an appreciation of the awesome power of collaborative intelligence."

Will Black, executive coach, SourceS of Executive Action

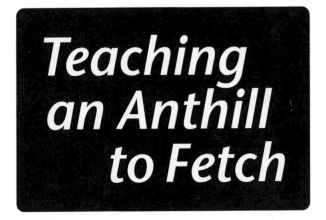

Teaching an Anthill to Fetch

*Developing Collaborative
Intelligence @ Work*

STEPHEN JAMES JOYCE

Mighty
Small
Books

 Stephen James Joyce, 2007

Attribution-NonCommercial-ShareAlike 2.5

You are free:

to Share — to copy, distribute and transmit the work

to Remix — to adapt the work

Under the following conditions:

Attribution. You must attribute the work in the manner specified by the author or licensor (but not in any way that suggests that they endorse you or your use of the work).

Noncommercial. You may not use this work for commercial purposes.

Share Alike. If you alter, transform, or build upon this work, you may distribute the resulting work only under the same or similar license to this one.

- For any reuse or distribution, you must make clear to others the license terms of this work.
- Any of the above conditions can be waived if you get permission from the copyright holder.
- Your fair use and other rights are in no way affected by the above. A complete version of this licence can be found at <www.creativecommons.org.>.

ISBN-10: 0-9780312-0-2
ISBN-13: 978-0-9780312-0-6

Printed and bound in Canada

First Printing

Library and Archives Canada Cataloguing in Publication

Joyce, Stephen James, 1959-

    Teaching an anthill to fetch : developing collaborative intelligence @ work / Stephen James Joyce.

Includes bibliographical references and index.
ISBN 978-0-9780312-0-6

1. Teams in the workplace. 2. Cooperativeness. 3. Group decision making. 4. Group problem solving. I. Title.

HD31.J69 2007   658.4'022   C2007-901053-9

Editor: Catherine Leek of Green Onion Pubishing
Interior Design and Electronic Page Composition: Kim Monteforte of
    WeMakeBooks.ca
Cover Design: Dianna Little
Cover Image: © Ron Elmy/Firstlight

Dedicated to Sandy, Zoey and Leland,
the most wonderful people in my life.
For all the love and joy you have given me.

Acknowledgments

A number of people gave me specific input that strengthened this work and I would like to thank them — Judy Kidd, Brian Woodward, Ken Lowe, Keith Webb, Don Hill, Gary McPherson, and Dan Dybl.

This book has taken form because of the excellent skill and guidance of a number of other people: my editor, Catherine Leek of Green Onion Publishing, who acted as mentor and editor and guided me through the process so gracefully; Kim Monteforte for her wonderful help with production and lay-out; Dianna Little for her patience and dedication and for creating a super cover design; and Jane Atkinson, my coach, for helping me to stay focused and "find my lane". Thanks guys it has been an enriching and joyful journey.

Finally to the most important person in the entire project — Sandy my highly talented and supportive partner. Without her this book would never have seen the light of day.

TABLE OF CONTENTS

A Word or Two About this Book

Teaching an Anthill to Fetch: Developing Collaborative Intelligence @ Work has been designed to be a practical tool for developing CQ in the workplace. Toward that end, we have provided a number of navigational tools.

There are a number of places throughout the book where we provide a "Go Deeper" feature. These are opportunities to explore the ideas covered in more depth through the Web site *www.anthillsite.com*. Here you will find web links connected to various topics.

CQ Tool© Exercises, called "CQ Tools", are placed at the end of each chapter. These are designed to develop deeper collaborative intelligence and will challenge and motivate you and your team.

An Introduction of Sorts

Ants, and all other insects that live in colonies, appear to be hard-wired to serve. By doing so, they ensure their survival. An anthill can survive and feed itself in some of the most hostile environments. No single ant knows how it all works — nor does it need to. Individually, ants are not that smart, but together they are very intelligent. The ant serves the anthill, which in turn serves the ant. The community the ants create and work to support is well equipped to cope with the challenge of change. In other words, the ant and the colony it belongs to is a good example of high level collaborative intelligence (CQ).

> **Collaborative Intelligence (CQ) is defined as the capacity to harness the intelligence in networks of relationships.**

Jim Donehey was the CEO of Capital One, the credit card company, when he coined the phrase, "You can't teach an anthill to fetch." He was referring to the task of helping his organization of 1800 people adapt and respond to a very competitive and rapidly changing marketplace. The challenge facing Doheney was how to focus the attention of the entire organization around vital business objectives.

Whether we are working inside a small team in a non-profit organization or in a large, multinational conglomerate, dealing with change is the ongoing challenge. Change forces us to adapt. Our adaptability defines how successful we are in dealing with change and how resilient we are.

Resilience is our ability to bounce back and recover from adverse conditions. It is the innate ability to respond resourcefully to challenges in our environment. Ray Kurzweil, author of *The Age of Spiritual Machines*, has calculated that the next century will be accompanied by 20,000 years of technological progress compared to today's rate of change. Therefore, our ability to adapt and respond to change is going to play a crucial role in the success of our species.

As the pressure to deal with change increases upon individuals, teams, and organizations, resilience will become more central to business. Tapping into individuals' and teams' natural resilience will become an essential element of business survival and success. As teams become increasingly virtual, productivity increases will be required; leadership skills will be demanded from more and more of the team's membership. Our capacity for resilience will be tested on a daily basis. However, when groups of people adapt and respond collectively incredible things happen. This is where collaborative intelligence becomes vital.

Nature is a vigorously adaptive system. The evolution of life is the history of adaptation. Ants have adapted to the challenge of building supportive colonies by applying some very simple rules. The argument of this book is that, for humans there are some simple "rules" that can enable us to work much more effectively together. These rules are much more like skills that we already have onboard and that we simply need to further enhance. Given the right circumstances, people and teams can embrace and develop these skills. By doing so, they are expanding their collaborative intelligence (CQ).

So What If You Could Teach an Anthill to Fetch?

This book takes a skill-building approach to the development of the CQ of teams. Each chapter ends with a skill-building exercise (CQ Tools©). The elements making up the development of CQ are:

1. Assumptions
2. Perception
3. Self-Mastery
4. Communication
5. Connection
6. Creativity/Flexibility
7. Meaningful Participation
8. "High CQ" Teams

We must begin within ourselves and so we begin in chapter 1 by checking **assumptions**. Choosing those ideas that will serve us and our team has a fundamental impact on the success of all other activities. Those assumptions will determine what sort of **perceptions** we have. Our perception of situations and other people affects how we respond to what happens to us. To adjust assumptions and manage our perceptions requires **self-mastery**. Self-mastery enables us to make the most of our personal resources. However, with all the self-mastery in the world, if we are unable to communicate effectively with others, we will be unable to affect the world around us.

Now we can move beyond ourselves to the bigger world and others. With great **communication** skills, we are able to build deep connection with others. Through **connection**, we create personal and team alignment, focusing our individual and group energies more effectively. This action raises productivity and helps create a stable team with higher levels of CQ. A team with deep and effective connection will be able to tap into greater levels of **creativity** and

flexibility. These can be further enhanced through skill-building exercises. Creative and flexible teams are able to adapt and respond to a rapidly changing environment.

When the going gets tough, people (and teams) need to know there is purpose to what they are trying to achieve. **Meaningful participation** provides a sense of purpose and direction.

The Chinese have a proverb, "May you live in interesting times." There is no debate that this has become true for us. How to deal with these interesting times is a lively and important debate. One thing is true, only when we can bring more of our CQ into play, will we be able to manage the levels of change occurring within business and society today. By increasing our collaborative intelligence, we truly are "teaching an anthill to fetch".

Assumptions

To a worm in horseradish,
the whole world is horseradish.

YIDDISH PROVERB

The sea squirt provides us a cautionary tale. When it is born, it floats through the open oceans seeking a place to make its home. Once the sea squirt finds a solid piece of ocean floor on which to attach itself, it does a peculiar thing. The sea squirt eats its brain. Having achieved its objective, a firm anchor within the ocean, it no longer needs its brain. You may know people like the sea squirt. They have a firm anchor in life or at work and, apparently, have long since consumed their brains. Zoologists say that the sea squirt shares 80% of our DNA. Some people probably share more than that. The sea squirt assumes that nothing is going to change in its environment and that it will no longer need to make significant adjustments. This may work for the sea squirt, but human beings can't afford to follow suit.

The Collective IQ Paradigm

Our society is changing rapidly. Intellectual intelligence (IQ) and emotional intelligence (EQ) are necessary but not sufficient in order to thrive in this world. Increasingly, we are expected to be able to harness the power of the group or network to achieve objectives. Collaborative intelligence, or CQ, has become increasingly important. The term "collaborative intelligence" was coined by William Isaacs in his book, *Dialogue and the Art of Thinking Together*. He defines CQ as the ability to build, contribute to and manage the power found in networks of people.

The development of our collaborative intelligence requires us to embrace a new paradigm. This new paradigm involves viewing all living things as deeply connected — an idea called "entanglement" in quantum mechanics. It follows then that there exists a collective intelligence to which we all contribute and to which, potentially, we all have access. Here is an example of what I mean. A room with 30 people in it, whose average age is 35, represents over 1000 years of life experience. Imagine the level of this team's CQ when processes that are designed to tap into the vast amount of collective life experience of this group are put into place.

Recently I worked with a group of mid-wives who had been experiencing some team challenges. In the past they had been a very resilient team, overcoming many significant challenges. More recently the team members had found themselves at odds with each other. Furthermore they had decided that a single individual was the source of all their problems. Rather than try to replace this person, the director decided to work with the team and attempt to resolve the issue. After the team had taken part in a facilitated dialogue around some of the pressing issues, they began to realize that they had all played a part in the circumstances leading up to the problems. Once this fact surfaced, they were able to explore exercises that enabled them to reconnect as a team. During a follow up session, it was reported that they had begun to function as a resilient team once more. We cannot begin to embrace a new paradigm unless we are willing to loosen our grip on the old one.

> *Acts of individual leadership are ineffective for changing a paradigm. It is a community-building process that must challenge and transform a collective worldview.*
> GOZDZ

Strengthening our CQ is more than simply learning to get along with each other. It requires that we begin to look at ourselves in a new way. It demands that we see ourselves as deeply interconnected with all of life and especially with all of humanity. Embracing this way of thinking will have noticeable effects on how management and teams operate. The significant challenges facing our societies can be overcome if we embrace our deep connection and then act accordingly.

The pressing issue is how do we tap into the CQ we all need as individuals and teams to meet the challenges of the future? At the most fundamental level, natural systems, of which we are a part, are cooperative rather than competitive. Competition takes place within the larger context of a highly cooperative system. In this way CQ is already a part of nature. As human beings, we express our collaborative intelligence in certain places, especially when we are placed in extremely challenging situations. Fire fighters, police officers, and emergency response teams, for example, report high levels of closely cooperative synchronized team behavior when things get tough. These are examples of CQ coming to the surface and enabling teams to behave resiliently. Throughout this book we will discover that CQ is a central tenet of all resilient systems, teams, and individuals.

Assumptions and Behaviors

If you try to change your behavior without first changing the underlying structure causing that behavior, you will not succeed. This is because structure determines behavior, not the other way around.
ROBERT FRITZ

One of the most persistent assumptions about business is that we can only prosper with a strong sense of competitiveness. Other companies in the same industry are viewed as the enemy to be beaten, out-maneuvered or destroyed. When we look closely at natural systems, however, we find a different story.

Fritjof Capra put it like this in *The Web of Life*, "Detailed study of ecosystems over the past decades has shown quite clearly that *most relationships between living organisms are essentially cooperative ones*, (my emphasis) characterized by coexistence and interdependence, and symbiotic in various degrees. Although there is competition, it usually takes place within a wider context of cooperation, so that the larger system is kept in balance." If natural systems hold the key to developing our own resilience, then we have to take a new look at the role competition and cooperation play in human systems (politics, business, etc.).

GO DEEPER
Natural Systems: www.anthillsite.com

Water — What Water?

Within the Zen tradition there is a story about two fish. One fish tells the other of a strange experience it had.

"I was swimming along and noticed a tasty morsel. I grabbed it, but a sharp, shiny, hard thing got stuck in my mouth. Suddenly, I was pulled from the water and the next thing I knew I was in a whole new world. A great big thing grabbed me and pulled the sharp, shiny, hard thing from my mouth and threw me back into the water."

The other fish looks shocked and asks, "Water? What water?"

The last animal to discover water would be a fish, just as we are the last ones to discover our assumptions about reality because we are so immersed in them.

> *ANY assumption can be made, but not all assumptions are created equal, and from their deductions you will know them.*
> JOHN EIDSER, *GLOBAL BRAIN*

Assumption — Checking as a Skill

The first of the seven skills that develop CQ and build resilient teams is *checking and adjusting individual and team assumptions*. Assumptions play such a central role in day-to-day life that, for the vast majority of time, we never notice them. One of the most important things assumptions do, however, is act as building blocks for our beliefs. There are a number of ways to change beliefs. One of the most effective ways is *check and adjust the assumptions* that support the belief.

It would be impossible to make it through the day without relying on some assumptions. Without them, life becomes much too complex. Doing the simplest things would become a series of complex decisions of nightmare proportions. Therefore, we have to make assumptions in order to get through each day.

How Did I Get Here?

We have all experienced the phenomenon of driving to work and wondering "How did I get here?" It is almost as if we were in a trance as we drove the well-known route. We were running on auto-pilot. Auto-pilot offers advantages and disadvantages. This highly-automated piece of our behavior may bring us predictable results, and some of those results may be highly desirable. Other results may be unwanted and problematic. For example, the auto-pilot you use to drive to your office enables you to plan the day ahead as you navigate the traffic. The downside is that when adjustments to the route are required — such as picking up a colleague on the way to work, it may not get done. Your auto-pilot wins over and your colleague loses out. Other times, you are the one who loses out. How many times have you found yourself driving to work when you had intended to make a trip to the store?

Individuals are not the only ones who can run on auto-pilot; teams can do it too. Supported by assumptions that go unchecked and unchallenged, teams can continue to run the same old routines for a long time before anyone notices what's happening. If the same old routine is getting you and your team the results you need, then that's a good thing. If not, then maybe it is time to lift the hood and have a peek into what's driving the team's behavior.

We all have experienced times when seemingly endless rounds of meetings produce no noticeable results. We find ourselves thinking that we've wandered into "Dilbert-land". The definition of insanity is doing the same thing over and over again expecting a different result. Many times the problem lies with unstated and unchallenged assumptions.

Good Servants But Bad Masters

Everyone I meet professionally for the first time receives a piece of string (it's threaded through my business card). The piece of string acts as a reminder for the story I share when they ask me what the piece of string represents.

I grew up on a 22-acre farm in the County of Down, Northern Ireland. When I was ten, my Dad sent me down to one of the pastures with a portable electric fence. He told me to fence the cows into a corner of the field. A few days later he came back and told me to go and take the fence down. "Use it to section off the bulls in the lower pasture," he said. "But Dad," I said, "what about the cows?" He said, "Oh just put a piece of string around them." I said, "A little piece of string isn't going to hold in a whole herd of cows." "Just do as you're told," was his reply.

So — liking life — I did as I was told and replaced the electric fence with a piece of string.

A few days later I went to check on the cows. They were standing in an area of scruffy, beaten down grass — hardly anything worth eating. All around them grew lush, green grass, and the only thing separating them from it was that flimsy piece of string and their belief that that piece of string would "shock" them.

> *What shocks me is that as intelligent human beings we often allow ourselves to be fenced in by a piece of string.*

What shocks me is that as intelligent human beings we often behave exactly like those cows. We allow ourselves to be fenced in by a piece of string — our beliefs. Rather than enabling us to live our lives fully, our beliefs often dictate what we can and cannot do. This is why I say that beliefs make good servants but bad masters. One of the most common mistakes we make is holding our beliefs to be true while refusing to accept all evidence to the contrary. This is the very definition of dogma.

Software of the Brain

Running in the background, beliefs (and the assumptions that help create them) act like the software of the brain. We don't notice them most of the time and usually only become aware of them when they begin to cause trouble, for example, when they prevent us from achieving things we really want. In presentations, I ask people to put their hands up if they like to be wrong. Understandably, there isn't much response to that request. The truth is, we all like to be right, and this is just as true when it comes to our beliefs. Like something to which we have habituated, we no longer notice them (water? What water?). We begin to treat those beliefs as if they were essential truths that really exist, rather than relative points of view that *we* adopted at some point in the past.

When your computer begins to cause trouble, once hardware issues have been ruled out, you *then* check the software running on the computer. So it is with our beliefs and assumptions. Just as there are typical things that cause software to malfunction, so there are certain types of beliefs that typically cause trouble.

Limitations of Our Beliefs

As remarkable as it is, even the human brain has its limitations. When we examine the types of beliefs that typically cause us trouble, we find they fall into three categories. We will briefly explore each of these now.

Hopelessness

In this case, the desired change is not possible, there is no hope. Take, for example, a physically handicapped man, who wishes to climb Mount Everest. Each time he thinks about the task, he also thinks no one who has his physical challenge has ever done it, so it's probably not possible — a wonderful dream, but hopeless. Another way of thinking about this type of belief is that the desired change is not possible for anyone; there is literally no hope.

Helplessness

In this instance, the desired change is possible for other people, just not for you. Our physically handicapped man may hear about someone else with a similar physical challenge who has climbed Everest. In this case, however, he might choose to believe that it was possible because someone else has achieved it, but he would not be capable. In other words, it's possible, but he feels personally helpless.

Worthlessness

Finally, in this situation the desired change is possible and you are capable of achieving it, but you are not worth it; you do not deserve the change. This is possibly the most tragic of the three types of limiting beliefs. In the case of the physically challenged person contemplating the ascent of Everest, he may have evidence that it is possible and that he does, indeed, have a chance at success. However, he doesn't think he is worthy or deserves to achieve it and so doesn't try (or try as hard as he should).

If you listen to people talk about their shattered hopes and unfulfilled desires, you will notice that most of the limiting beliefs in operation fall into one of these three categories. The point in categorizing the beliefs is that if you can spot the type of limiting belief in operation, you can make the appropriate adjustments to overcome it.

Challenging These Limitations

A simple way to dislodge a hopelessness belief is to "act as if" it were possible. Roger Bannister acted as if it were possible to break the four-minute mile barrier. He also trained accordingly, rather than sitting around waiting to see what would happen. In this case actions really can change beliefs.

In the case of a limiting belief related to helplessness, one of the best ways to address it is by searching out a counter example. That is, look for those who have already achieved the thing — after all, they are living proof that the objective is attainable. Looking to our heroes (sporting or otherwise) can be useful for finding appropriate models.

Beliefs related to worthlessness require that we check the deeper reasons we feel unworthy of the desired goal and address that issue. Self-esteem is often underestimated in relation to the powerful effect it can have on our performance. Negative messages received when we were children often determine what we think we deserve and, until they have been checked and adjusted, will continue to do so.

The Santa Clause

If you grew up in North America, you probably believed in Santa Claus when you were a child. This is "beliefs stage one" where you believe everything that you are told. As you grew older you discovered, usually from older kids, that Santa Claus didn't exist. This is "beliefs stage two" where you realize that some things you are told are true and some are not, and it is your task to decide which is which. As you got older and had children of your own, you probably told them about Santa Claus and helped them create that fantasy. This is "beliefs stage three" — you have now *become* Santa Claus (which is why I call it the Santa "Clause"). You realize at this point that some beliefs can be useful, even if they are created. At another level, you may even realize that all beliefs are created. Creating the belief in Santa Claus was a beneficial thing. The belief enables children and parents to take part in a centuries-old tradition involving ritual, mystery, and fantasy. However, holding onto the original kind of belief about

> *All beliefs are created and, therefore, can be changed.*

Santa Claus (that he is a real person with a very unusual sleigh and so forth) into adulthood would not be very useful.

Reality Is What We Notice

What we assume about life has a fundamental effect on the way we interact with it. Everyone knows at least one person who has a very negative view of life. Such people expect the worst and often they are not disappointed. Their success in predicting the worst is based in part on the connection between *intention* and *attention*. That is, our attention is directed by our intention. There is a portion of our nervous system that plays a role in connecting intention and attention. It is called the ascending reticular activating system (aRAS) and it is located in the brainstem. The aRAS acts as a pattern recognition system and strongly affects the brain's arousal. The way this part of the brain works helps to explain how our thoughts manifest into reality.

Best-selling author Gary Zukav explains the process succinctly, as follows: "Reality is what we take to be true. What we take to be true is what we believe. What we believe is based upon our perceptions.

What we perceive depends upon what we look for. What we look for depends upon what we think. What we think depends upon what we perceive. What we perceive determines what we believe. What we believe determines what we take to be true. What we take to be true is our reality."

In other words, the assumptions we make about reality play a large part in creating that reality. We make so many assumptions that we cease to be aware of them. Becoming aware of the basic assumptions we use can be a tricky process. Seeing through our assumptions about reality is an important part of becoming enlightened in many of the great spiritual traditions such as Sufi and Zen. There, stories and puzzles (known as *koans* in Zen) are used to enable students to break out of limiting assumptions about reality. The story line of the movie *The Matrix* (based on the very same ideas and the principles themselves) dates back thousands of years.

GO DEEPER
Assumptions about Reality: www.antihillsite.com

What Do Assumptions Have to Do with CQ?

What we assume about ourselves, life, and other people has a tremendous impact on how we operate as human beings. Consider the central assumption about resilience — *that we are all inherently resilient.* This assumes everyone has resilience as an onboard capacity. Making this assumption affects the attitude we take toward ourselves and the way we treat others. In turn this affects the level of CQ we can tap into.

Many organizations already operate on this assumption of resilience with regard to employee development. An example is

Appreciative Inquiry (AI). AI is an organizational development approach that assumes it is more effective to concentrate on what is working within an individual, team, and company, rather than on what is not working. A core principle within the Appreciative Inquiry model is questioning assumptions. Practitioners of AI report that once the questioning process has begun, people become inspired to question other previously unquestioned assumptions. Such questioning is a crucial first step to any real change within organizations. The shared assumptions of a group or team have a very strong effect. Helping a team become aware of its shared assumptions can be the single most important source of positive change. Some organizational development programs bring in their own processes and assumptions. Rather than layering on another set, it makes more sense to discover what assumptions (useful or not-so-useful) have created the system that is in operation now.

Self-Fulfilling Prophets and Losses

Assumptions easily become self-fulfilling prophesies (or profits and losses when they operate within a business). They act as filters on our perceptions, and we literally see what we have programmed ourselves to look for. In turn, our perceptions of events will determine our own responses. Our responses have specific effects and usually provide further evidence to support the original assumption.

For example, suppose you suspected someone (made an assumption about them) of being dishonest. This assumption would cause you to filter all your observations of that person for dishonest behaviors. This affects the other person, who may wish to reassure you that he is honest. The more the person tries to convince you of his trustworthiness, the more you become convinced that he has something to hide. The original assumption about his dishonesty enabled you to redefine the meaning of his behavior. Voilá — the power of self-fulfilling prophesies!

Figure 1.1
The Self-Fulfilling Prophesy Cycle

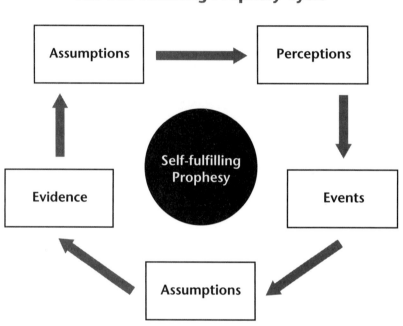

What Do You Believe about the Problem?

It is very tempting, when faced with a problem, to stop and ask "What *do* I or we need to do to solve this problem?" This question addresses the challenge at the level of behavior and, although there is no harm in this question, it does not get at the deeper issues. A more fundamental and useful question to ask is, "What do I need to *believe* in order to solve this problem?" Maybe we are having difficulty with someone who reports to us or with someone to whom we report. It is useful to ask, "What assumptions am I making about this situation/person?" Often, we discover that something we are assuming is helping to create the problem in the first place.

It's easy for us to develop assumptions that limit our resilience. For example: "this team won't support me" (so you never ask for it); "that person hates me" (so we look for evidence to support that); "I can't achieve this objective" (which affects how much effort we put in). I am sure you can think of many more you use with yourself and others.

Gary McPherson — A Testament to the Power of Assumptions

Gary McPherson's life is a testament to the power of assumptions. Gary was a fun-loving, athletic nine-year-old boy when, in 1955, he was struck down with Polio.

For the next 34 years of his life, Gary would live in hospital and would require the use of a ventilator that would allow him to breath. In the early days of his illness, many of the medical staff around him continued to believe that Gary would not survive. Yet over the years, Gary continued to defy the odds, even as he lost many of his friends from the ward in which he lived. He discovered that some people with his condition had learned to "frog breath", a method of drawing air into the lungs without using the diaphragm. Gary identifies this as the single most important thing he did that enabled him to regain a certain amount of his independence. No longer dependent on a ventilator to breathe for 24 hours at a time, Gary had managed to wrestle more freedom for himself and he left the hospital at age 43 while continuing to use a wheelchair for mobility.

Gary explains that in the early stages of his hospitalization, he heard that life expectancy for someone with his condition was five years. He recalls living his life in five-year increments and being surprised when he reached his fourteenth and nineteenth birthdays. By this time, he explains, he felt pretty good and began to think, "well I'm still alive, maybe I should think about doing some things".

When talking to Gary, you quickly get a sense of someone who is focused on what he can do, as opposed to what he can't. The *assumptions* Gary uses are based around possibility and persistence. He confesses that he negotiates with himself around what he can shoot for and then decides upon the increments for which he will aim.

Gary didn't set out as a 19-year old, almost totally paralyzed by Polio, to become the Executive Director of the Canadian Centre for Social Entrepreneurship. Nor did he envision himself playing a key role in shaping services for people with disabilities in Alberta. Serving eight years as the President of the Canadian Wheelchair Sports Association (CWSA) was not on his mind either. In the early years of his illness, Gary probably never imagined he would become an adjunct professor or guest lecturer with an Honorary Doctor of Law degree. However, *his assumptions* about his situation and the options open to him supported each small step toward an amazing career.

Gary is now married with two teenage children and talks about entering politics. He says that because his kids are older, he has more time on his hands. It is a truly humbling experience to sit and chat with Gary as he talks about plans for the future. Most of them are centered upon what he can help others achieve.

In conversation, Gary is quick to mention the powerful effect assumptions have had in his life. The assumption that by serving others we heal ourselves has helped Gary to make significant contributions to society. Along with that is the assumption that you can find humor in everything. It is difficult to sit very long with Gary without being drawn into his expansive sense of humor. His philosophy of life has a central assumption that has become a mantra for Gary — "You see what you look for — so choose carefully what you look for."

Amid all the committees and commitments Gary undertook he still found time to write the story about his battle and eventual victory against tremendous odds. *With Every Breath I Take* sheds light on the heart and spirit of a remarkable man.

GO DEEPER

Gary McPherson: www.anthillsite.com

A great deal of anecdotal evidence demonstrates that people are able to sustain themselves in challenging conditions and situations. There are definable traits that can be identified, and we all have them. This book explores a specific set of skill-building exercises that make it possible for us to develop these traits further. In the process we expand our CQ.

Assumptions About Resilience

Since this chapter is devoted to an exploration of assumptions, it makes sense to state clearly some of the assumptions that underpin the approach taken in this book.

- Change is a constant process.
- Our ability to adapt to change is the central role of resiliency.
- Resiliency is the ability to adapt, bounce back, and recover in harsh or challenging conditions.
- Resiliency is an innate capacity that we all have.
- Certain definable traits make up our capacity for resilience.

- Traits of resilience have been identified and we are able to strengthen them further with specific exercises.
- Resilient teams are built from resilient individuals.
- None of us are as smart as all of us — a resilient team further strengthens its individual members.
- Everyone wants to make a difference with their lives. Work is a great place for that to happen.

Exercises that challenge you to re-assess what you assume about certain things will enable you and your team to become aware of the dangers of auto-pilot thinking.

Just as limiting assumptions can cause all sorts of problems to the individual and team, a well thought-out and consciously chosen assumption can be equally liberating and empowering. Prior to May 6, 1954, it was assumed that the four-minute mile was impossible. Roger Banister forced everyone to revise that assumption. The revised assumption generated a new belief.

> *[Red Queen] "Let's consider your age to begin with — how old are you?"*
> *"I'm seven and a half, exactly."*
> *"You needn't say 'exactly'," the Queen remarked.*
> *"I can believe it without that. Now I'll give you something to believe. I'm just one hundred and one, five months and a day."*
> *"I can't believe that!" said Alice.*
> *"Can't you?" the Queen said in a pitying tone. "Try again: draw a long breath, and shut your eyes."*
> *Alice laughed. "There's no use trying," she said, "one can't believe impossible things."*
> *"I daresay you haven't had much practice," said the Queen. "When I was your age, I always did it for*

half an hour a day. Why, sometimes I've believed as
many as six impossible things before breakfast."
LEWIS CARROLL, *THROUGH THE LOOKING GLASS*

Joseph Campbell, authority on world mythology, once stated that many people reach the top of the ladder only to find it leaning against the wrong wall. I would like to add that there are two other types of ladders: the ladder that was chosen too short for the desired effect (right wall, ladder not long enough) and the ladder lying on the ground (uncommitted to anything, it serves no one, and may actually trip someone.) Consciously choosing beliefs and assumptions that will serve you in your life is like choosing a ladder. It is important to lean it against the right wall and aim it in the right direction for you.

> *You need to ask yourself,*
> *"Is your ladder leaning*
> *against the right wall*
> *and is it long enough?"*

Once positioned, ask yourself if the ladder is long enough. Is your belief strong enough to enable you to achieve your goal? Have you committed yourself to achieving the goal? Have you actually leaned your ladder against the wall? In other words, have you committed to do something about the belief you have chosen?

Good Questions Rather than Easy Answers

Asking questions is something few of us developed as a skill as we grew up. For most of us, our educational experience consisted of being told to remember the right answer. The focus was clearly on the production of answers to a relatively fixed set of questions (tests and exams). There was little attention given to the creation of good questions. Yet, throughout history, practically all of the major scientific breakthroughs came from people who were fascinated with a particular question and all the possible answers, rather than a search for one right answer. Einstein asking himself what it would be like to ride a beam of light brought him to one of the greatest discoveries of the 20th century — the theory of relativity.

Using the right set of assumptions has a huge impact on our level of resilience. Asking good questions is an important step toward checking our assumptions about our own resilience. Testing what assumptions are presently running means asking the right questions. Questions direct our curiosity and our energy.

Best-selling author Peter Block claims that "we define...our future through the questions we choose to address." In chapter 4 we will look at the topic of questions in much greater detail and more specifically how they can enrich our communication (and, therefore, connection) with our team.

Hitting a "Whole" in One

Increasingly, people are seeking fulfillment in the non-material, psychological, and spiritual aspects of life. This movement up Maslow's hierarchy of needs applies to life in general, but also to work. More and more employees and team members wish to "transform themselves" personally as well as professionally.

There is an outstanding opportunity for companies who are willing to offer their employees training and development opportunities that help grow the whole person. It could also be viewed as a chance for the company to evolve their people from the inside out.

Many companies have already seized the opportunity to grow their people in this way. In Nancy and Kevin Freiburg's book, *Guts*, John Mackey, CEO of the Whole Foods Company, is quoted as saying, "I don't see any conflict between wearing our hearts on our sleeves and running a company that is serious about profits. In fact we feel there is a profound synergy between the two. Both are about responsibility." By walking its talk, Whole Foods has gained a place on *Fortune*'s list of the 100 best companies to work for in the U.S. six years running.

WHERE WE'VE BEEN

- The assumptions we make deeply affect our personal and professional lives.
- Our beliefs are created from our assumptions.
- Group assumptions are at play within teams at all times.
- To create sustainable, lasting change, we must identify the assumptions behind our behaviors.
- All beliefs are created, therefore all beliefs can be changed.
- Good questions are a great way to challenge and change limiting beliefs.
- Successful business operations and teams are based on useful assumptions/beliefs.

WHERE WE'RE GOING

The assumptions we make and the beliefs that radiate out from them have a profound effect on the way we see the world. Our perceptions are colored by what we think. The next chapter will show how perception plays a central role in the unconscious processes of resilient individuals. We will also look at how important perception is in building resilient teams and how developing CQ relies on how we see just as much as what we see.

Questions to consider are:

- What assumptions could you make that would transform your own resilience and that of your team?
- What shared assumptions would enable your team/place of work to become an adaptive, vibrant center for human and business growth?

The following exercises will enable you and your team to explore important questions such as these.

CQ Tool© 1

Checking Assumptions

Checking assumptions can be a very important first step before a team launches into a project together. In many cases it negates the need to stop later and discover that members' assumptions are working at odds with each other.

The following exercise enables team members to explore the assumptions that may be in operation as the team gathers (metaphorically speaking) around a task or project.

Note: for purposes of this exercise a context has been chosen. You may wish to use this as a "practice session" and move onto a more pertinent issue once you and your team feel they have mastered the stages and process.

STAGE ONE: The team is divided into groups of four to eight. Each group places a piece of flip chart paper upon the wall in landscape format. Divide the page into three equal columns. The heading "Assumptions" is written at the top of the middle column.

STAGE TWO: Give the project team the task of brainstorming a list of assumptions for planning a team retreat (e.g., that it must be out of town, it must be held during weekdays, etc.). A specific and short time period (five to ten minutes) is allowed for this stage.

STAGE THREE: The team is asked to choose between three and five of the most interesting or controversial assumptions and circle them (one minute for this task).

STAGE FOUR: Write the word "Valid" into the header of the right-hand column. They are now asked to use the chosen assumptions to explore whether the implications/consequences of these assumptions are valid. In short, answer the question "What if they were valid?" (five to seven minutes for this task).

STAGE FIVE: The group is asked to place the word "Invalid" as the heading for the final (left-hand) column. Exploring the same chosen assumptions, this time answering the question "What are the implications/consequences if these assumptions were invalid?" (five to seven minutes for this step).

STAGE SIX: The group is asked to reflect upon the exercise and comment upon what they noticed. Some questions the facilitator can use at this point are:

- What did you notice about your own assumptions?
- Were you surprised by some of the assumptions other people had?
- If you had the opportunity to explore the invalid options of assumptions you agreed with what effect did that have?
- How could this process help teams form strategies around a project?

Perception

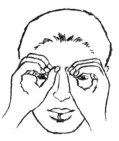

*It's never enough just to tell people about
some new insight… Instead of pouring
knowledge into people's heads; you need to
help them grind a new set of eyeglasses
so they can see the world in a new way.*

JOHN SEELY BROWN

In chapter 1, we explored how assumptions affect the adaptability and resilience of you and your team. We also considered how relative perception really is. Our reality is based upon what we notice, which in turn is heavily based upon our assumptions. Our assumptions provide stability to the reality that we create on a moment-by-moment basis. The process is largely unconscious. However, even when we do change our assumptions about things, we retain our old *ways of looking at things*. We continue to wear our old prescription as it were.

This chapter is about how we look at things, about how our perception affects our resilience. We will also explore how our perception and awareness affect our ability to collaborate with others. In other words, how we perceive others will determine whether we choose to collaborate or not. To this extent our perceptions determine our collaborative intelligence.

In this chapter we will examine five important elements of perception.

1. **Attention** can be harnessed and focused — our attention affects our experience of our life.
2. **Perception** as an active process — what we see depends on where we look.
3. **Filters** can be changed — they select the information that reaches the conscious mind.
4. **Perspectives** change our awareness — the perspective we take determines what we see.
5. **Frames** can help us become more flexible — how we frame our perceptions affects the meaning we form.

> *Difficulties strengthen the mind, as labour does the body.*
> SENECA

Changing perceptions has had a huge impact on my own life. In 1995, while living in Northern Ireland, I was involved in a road accident that almost cost me my life. I was standing beside my car on a narrow country road, when a speeding car skidded on black ice and rammed into my parked car. The force of the crash pushed my car over top of me. Miraculously I slid under my car as it glided over the road — I "came to" lying underneath it. It was still on its wheels and I had somehow slipped through the space between the car and the ground.

Months later the full impact of the accident was discovered. A disc in my back had been torn apart by the injury and a consultant was explaining to me that I had degenerative disc disease. I was told that the condition "will only get worse". (Now, there is a nice belief system.) He offered to speed up the process for me to receive a handicapped sticker!

Maybe you can imagine what I felt like as I walked (painfully) out of his office. What the consultant had said was slowly sinking in. He had inadvertently helped me form a perception of myself as a "cripple". I mentally formed a long list of things I could no longer do because of my injury. A number of years passed as I lived my life surrounded by things I couldn't do because of my back.

I was living a "half life", both personally and professionally. What I didn't realize was that the assumptions I had created as a result of my conversations with medical staff had left me with very strong (and limiting) filters through which I perceived my life. There was no particular moment of "enlightenment". Instead, an evolution of frustration brought me to a point where I realized I had to change.

I decided I needed to *do* something to prove to myself that I was capable of moving beyond my injury. If I threw my heart over the fence, I thought, the rest of me might well follow.

Then one day I heard of a group of people planning a hike in the Andes in Chile, South America. This had been a life-long ambition of mine. Images of the glaciers and watching condors sail over head occupied my mind.

The next day I went to see a personal trainer in the local gym. I asked him if he knew anyone with my sort of injury that still worked out. He said he had quite a few clients. I signed up and started with small exercises. At that time I could not stand up for longer than ten minutes without my right leg going numb and intense pain in my lower back. With great professional advice from Paul, my trainer, and lots of physical training on my behalf I was able to make the trip to Chile. The transition from "cripple to climber" was brought about by a change in how I perceived myself. Sounds simple!

However I had to *do* a number of things to help the change take place in my self-perception. I realized that wishing alone would not change anything.

1. Attention

Three pounds of tofu hidden inside a bone box; you could eat it with a spoon and it's the most important thing in your life. It's your brain of course and its only connection with the outside world is a set of senses that feed it information. The human nervous system is amazing. Through our five senses we process approximately 11 million pieces of information every second. Our eyes send 10 million signals to the brain each second and together have more computing power than six Cray computers connected together.

> Q: *Three pounds of tofu in a bone box?*
> A: *Your brain.*

So of what is our brain capable? Researchers in this field have attempted to calculate how much information we can process consciously, but by all estimates it is not much. The most optimistic figure is 40 pieces out of the 11 million pieces per second (Tor Norretranders, *The User Illusion*).

Up Periscope

One way of thinking about how this vast amount of information gets filtered to a small fraction is to think about our conscious mind as a periscope. Our lives are effectively made up of those 40 pieces multiplied by the number of seconds we live. Where we point the periscope determines our awareness. The auto-pilots mentioned in chapter 1 come into play here. They determine, to a large degree, where we habitually direct our attention. In order to tap into greater depths of our own resilience, we will have to revisit these old patterns of perceiving; check the settings on the auto-pilots. Are they optimal for where we want to end up?

All great athletes know that their performance is highly dependent on where they place their attention. A good sports coach spends a lot of time working in this area, helping the athlete to harness his or her attention. The old eastern expression "energy flows where attention goes", implies that our energy follows our attention. What we attend to grows and proliferates. Often we believe that it is the things we are not attending to that cause us trouble. Frequently it is the other way around. So when you or your team is faced with a particular challenge it may be useful to stop and ask, "What are we attending to that has helped us create this problem?"

"Rubber–necking" is a great example of this phenomenon. It is defined as the tendency to look at accidents to the extent that you become one. According to the American Automobile Association, between 25 and 55% of all road accidents are caused by distracted drivers. We have all seen other people do it and, in all probability, we have been guilty of doing it many times ourselves. We give our attention to an accident we are passing and don't attend properly to the road ahead. With only so much attention at our disposal, splitting our attention means we have less available to devote to driving our own car. This principle is also important when we are dealing with challenges either individually or in teams. Directing our attention is vital when we need to have our energy flow in a certain direction.

> *"What are we attending to that has helped us create this problem?"*

Questions are a great way to focus your attention. You can help your team members direct their attention by asking the right questions. One of the differences between a good team leader and a great one is that a good team leader asks some good questions (rather than providing easy answers) and a great team leader asks great questions (and supports the team in forming their own answers).

Although there is a large unconscious component in how we organize our attention, we can, with conscious control, move our attention. Meditative practices are really attention-training systems. This is one of the reasons meditation can be so helpful in building emotional balance. You are effectively training yourself to control your own attention. Our society has become a noisy place to live in — with many distractions and advertisers clamoring to catch and hold our attention for as long as possible. Our attention is a precious resource that we must look after carefully otherwise it can be hijacked or dissipated by external forces.

> *Unless a person knows how to give order to his or her thoughts, attention will be attracted to whatever is most problematic at the moment: it will focus on some real or imaginary pain, on recent grudges or long-term frustrations. Entropy is the normal state of consciousness — a condition that is neither useful nor enjoyable.*
> MIHALY CSIKSZENTMIHALYI, *FLOW*

The quote from Mihaly Csikszentmihalyi conveys the need to use our attention as a form of energy. By channeling attention toward something useful, we are doing two things: 1) Not allowing any of our valuable energy to be wasted on harmful or wasteful activities; and 2) we are bringing it all to bear upon the important task of creating what we do want to happen.

GO DEEPER

Attention: www.anthillsite.com

Team mission statements can serve the same function. They help the team members harness the collective attention around specific objectives, drawing people around a common purpose.

Many businesses go to a great deal of trouble to create visions for their company. One of the benefits of a business vision is that it focuses attention on what is important to the company. Ideally the business vision orchestrates the attention (and energy) of the whole organization.

Our resilience is dependent, in part, upon how we use our energy. Therefore how we organize attention will have a large impact on our resilience. Mihaly Csikszentmihalyi, in his book *Flow: The Psychology of Optimal Experience*, goes so far to say that "attention is our most important tool in the task of improving the quality of experience." When I think of directing attention what comes to my mind are images of cairns (piles of stones) that people build to show the path up a mountain. In a similar way the Inuit people have used special rock formations called "Inukshuk" for centuries as a way of pointing the traveler's attention along a safe route.

This chapter is about building cairns to harness our own attention with the purpose of establishing a more optimal experience. By marshaling our attention we will be more resilient. Exploring this process as a team will enable your team to harness its *collective attention*. The result will be a more resilient team.

2. Perception Is Projection

How we see things has a great deal to do with how we feel about things. When we have strong emotions about something we often project these outward onto events that are occurring around us. For example, if I become angry about something in the morning, I may notice many other things during my day that also make me angry. Emotions have powerful affects on what we notice. It is a common misconception that perception is a passive process carried out by our senses. The scientific evidence points to perception being an *active* process closely tied to the flow of our emotions. Choosing how to view an event is one of the secrets of emotional mastery. (We will visit this topic in greater detail in chapter 3.)

> *Enlightenment is waking up to the illusions contained in the belief we have been fed since birth: the belief that whether or not we are at peace depends upon what we have or do in the material world. It is discovering for oneself, as a personal experience of life, that whether or not we are at peace depends on our perception and interpretation of events.*
> PETER RUSSELL

When Captain Cook first arrived on the shores of what is now North America, the Arawak Indians were reported to be unable to see his ships. What they saw we will never know, however, the principle has modern examples much closer to home. A young woman who moved from the Philippines to North America did not recognize that some of the people she was meeting had red hair (she had never met someone with that color of hair in her home country). It was such an uncommon sight in her native land that she was literally unable to "see it". Months later she began to notice that some people had a hair color that was new to her. She then began to notice that even people she was very close to in her new country had red hair. The distinction for red hair had not been important where she had grown up and it took some time for her perceptual system to rewire for its existence.

These are rather dramatic examples of a process that is going on inside each of us all the time. We see things when we are ready to see them. This has an impact on how resilient we are. For example, what might you not be seeing that is going on within your team or life, for that matter? Are some limiting assumptions "invisible" because we have not looked for them? Shifts in what we can see come with shifts in our awareness. The exercises at the end of this chapter are designed to cause shifts in your awareness. In doing so they will enable you to see things differently.

But what has the story of the invisible ships got to do with our resilience? Maturana and Varela are well-known researchers in the field of physiological psychology. They have demonstrated that our perceptions are heavily biased toward the use of already-on-board information. In other words our perceptions at any particular moment in time are based on 20% *new* information — fresh from the environment, so to speak — and a whooping 80% of *onboard* information. The 80% represents information our nervous system has stored about the environment. Our nervous system patches together the

20% new and 80% old to create an experience of *reality*. Such a recipe of sources leaves us very prone to errors.

Optical illusions are great examples of how easily our nervous system is fooled. Look at the illustration in Figure 2.1 and notice how easy it is to see a white triangle that is not there?

Figure 2.1
Can You See a White Triangle?

The white triangle in Figure 2.1 is caused by a combination of the 80% of onboard information and the 20% new information. Our brain is attempting to make sense of the image and completes it for us. This particular illusion also can be used to explain how our assumptions help build our reality.

Now in Figure 2.2, each of the little pies represents an assumption/belief that we have onboard. Our brains complete the picture for us and assure us that the space in the middle is reality. Within every team there is a "reality" being created by the shared assumptions of all its members. These in turn shape our perceptions that we then take to be our "reality". If a team wishes to change its reality, then the assumptions and perceptions need to be examined first.

Figure 2.2
Is the White Triangle Clearer?

Assumption 1

'Reality'

Assumption 3   **Assumption 2**

What You See Is What You Choose to See

Being able to shift our attention from one perception to another is known as "perceptual flexibility". Perceptual flexibility can be demonstrated using the necker tube experiment.

Figure 2.3
Necker Tube Experiment

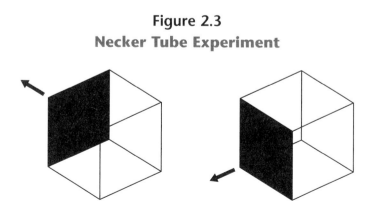

Look at Figure 2.3 and notice which plane seems to be the one closest to you. Now bring the other plane up into the foreground and allow the first plane you chose to fall into the background. Some of you may be struggling; others will find it a very simple task. With a little effort you will be able to switch the tube between the two perspectives. Typically once someone has done this they will be able to choose the kind of tube they see. This is an example of how we express our perceptual flexibility.

So far we've discovered that our reality is a construct. Physicists assure us that the concept of a solid physical world "out there" is, at best, a nice idea not supported by research. Philosopher and physicist David Bohm often said, "Thought creates the world and then says, 'I didn't do it.'"

This can be unnerving and reassuring depending upon how you look at it (there's that perspective thing again). The world we live in was created and is continually being created, to a large extent, by what goes on in our own nervous system. This further emphasizes the ancient wisdom that if we wish to change the world we must first change ourselves.

And yet it is so tempting to point outward to all those things (including people) that are the cause of the problem. It's even more attractive when it is a team of people that is not performing well or an organization that is functioning poorly. The implications for anyone in a position of leadership are pretty obvious so I won't labor this point.

 **GO DEEPER**
Perceptions: www.anthillsite.com

3. Filtered or Instant?

With the massive amount of information arriving at our nervous system from the outside, it's not surprising that our brain has to filter it. Effectively our nervous system is tuned to notice some things and ignore a lot of others. The software running this process is informed by filters for dangerous things. Once our basic needs — things we can eat, drink or mate with — have been satisfied, or dangers safely avoided, a different set of filters become active. These are designed to search for ways that higher needs can be satisfied, for example those related to social belonging and self-esteem. Maslow's hierarchy of needs shows one possible set of filters that our nervous system can sort with.

GO DEEPER

Maslow's Hierarchy of Needs: www.anthillsite.com

We could view filters as one of the reasons goal-setting is such a successful process. By setting goals we are setting intention. Setting intention is like programming our nervous system to filter for things that are important to our goals in the environment.

Perceptual filters are just as active in the workplace as they are outside it. They determine, to a great extent, how we perceive others. There are a wide range of personality profiling systems that provide insight into how people behave. When someone is profiled as an "INFJ" or a "strong blue", that label is used to explain why they are the way they are. With this set of filters personality is very often conceived as a static thing that changes little. The concept of *character* and *building character* is often not factored into how companies manage their human resources. In real life we know people do change, either through self-directed re-invention or as a result of events occurring in their lives (for example becoming a father or mother). Profiling systems, like all filters, can have liberating and restricting effects.

GO DEEPER
Building Character: www.anthillsite.com

For a long time psychologists have known about the Fundamental Attribution Error (FAE). When interpreting other people's behavior FAE causes us to over-estimate the importance of basic personality traits and under-estimate the significance of situation and context. In this case the filter for personality traits is stronger than those for situation or context. Simply put, FAE causes us to form stereotypes and can lead to various forms of bias. Sexism, racism, and ageism are examples of biased perceptions. We tend to see what we want to see. Optical illusions are a great example of how unreliable our perceptions can be (see Figures 2.1 to 2.2).

> *We do not see the world as it is, we see it as we are.*
> MARCUS AURELIUS

If we wish to change the world (or another person or a team) we must first ask, "what changes do we need to make within ourselves?" Choosing to look at a person or situation from a more productive perspective will automatically enhance our CQ. By looking for places where collaboration is possible we will find more.

Being able to restructure our perceptions of reality is a fundamental aspect of our own innate resilience. Social psychologists Daniel Gilbert and Timothy Wilson suggest that we have our own "psychological immune system" that acts to protect us from threats to our (psychological) well-being. "When it comes to maintaining a sense of well-being," they say, "each of us is the ultimate spin doctor." The ability to put a spin on our perceptions can just as easily hold us stuck as liberate us. This is where assumptions (especially about ourselves) have such an impact on perception.

4. Perspective — What We Find Depends on Where We Look

Within the Sufi tradition there are many stories about a mystic joker called Mulla Nasrudin. One such story relates how a good friend finds the Mulla on a dark night on his hands and knees underneath a street lamp crying. His friend enquires why he is crying. The Mulla explains he has just lost his gold coins; his life savings are gone. The friend immediately feels sorry for the Mulla and gets down on the ground to help look for the coins. After a period of fruitless searching the friend gets up and asks, "Mulla can you remember where you were standing when you dropped your coins?" "Oh yes," replies the Mulla. "I was down there in that dark alleyway." "Why in heavens name are you looking under the street lamp then?" his exasperated friend asks. "Because there is more light here," the Mulla replies.

I find this story funny and tragic at the same time. The Mulla is doing exactly what we do so often. He is looking for the answer where there is the most light rather than where he really knows the answer lies. More specifically I have often attempted

> *Optimal perception is as much about where you look as it is about how you look.*

to find the cause of some problem in the environment — out there — rather than looking where I knew the problem to lie — inside myself. The knack to optimal perception is not only how we look but also where.

It Looked Bigger in the Store

Colin Turnbull, in his book *The Forrest People*, relates a story about a Pygmy he had befriended while traveling through the African continent. This Pygmy had lived his entire life in the thick jungles of East Africa. Turnbull took the Pygmy to the Serengeti, the great open plains that border the jungle and showed him the wild life of the plains. The life-long forest dweller asked, "what insects are those?" referring to the water buffalo that were a long distance away. When he was informed that the "insects" were water buffalo he laughed out loud and called Turnbull a liar. The Pygmy's perceptual world was biased so heavily toward the short distances of tropical jungle life that he could not conceive that these buffalo were real.

The environment in which we live and work undoubtedly affects our capacity to see. We become accustomed to the perspectives available and don't even realize that we have been conditioned. Therefore anything that enables us to change our perspectives will inevitably change what we are able to see.

An Elephant by Any Other Name

This is not the only way that our perceptions can be restricted. I am sure you are familiar with the story of the six blind men around the elephant. This story originated in the eastern philosophical tradition and is a metaphor about reality and our own incomplete grasp of it. Each of the six blind men touch a different part of the elephant and the zoo keeper asks them what they think an elephant is. The blind man holding onto the trunk says that an elephant is a snake-like thing; the one holding onto the ear, a fan-like thing; and so it goes on, each of the blind men defining the elephant by the part of its anatomy with which they are familiar.

From a psychological perspective we have at least three perspectives we can use to view our own reality. The *first position* is the perspective of us standing in our own physical space, looking out through our own eyes. This perspective is also associated with using words like "I", "me", and "myself" when referring to our feelings. When we describe an experience from the first position we tend to re-experience the feelings of the event as if we were in our own body. Typically when we think of the event we do not see ourselves in images of the experience.

The *second position* is being able to assume someone else's perspective in an experience. We take on the other's perspective seeing and hearing what they see and hear. When we explore this perspective deeply we will also be able to imagine what they feel like. This perspective is the basis of empathy and can be a powerful tool in discovering what it is like to be another person. One of the greatest benefits of this perspective is that it enables us to understand the other person's world better and to communicate more effectively with them. The experience is often described as "walking a mile in their shoes".

The *third position* is characterized by the fact that we are not associating with anyone in the situation. We are not assuming the perspective of being inside our own body, nor are we imagining being in the body of anyone else. The perspective is that of "a fly on the wall" floating free from feelings and able to observe events and the behaviors of ourselves and others in a totally detached way. This is a very effective perspective to take when we wish to separate ourselves from our own individual feelings and the feelings of others.

None of the perspectives is any better than the other. They all serve a useful function. People who explore all three perspectives of an event are better informed than someone who explores only one (typically first position). Exploring all the perspectives is also described as using perceptual flexibility.

Once again the three perceptual positions are:

1. First Position — looking through our own eyes;
2. Second Position — stepping into someone else's shoes and looking through their eyes; and
3. Third Position — viewing the situation as if we were a disembodied eye witness or "fly on the wall".

Most of us have a preferred perceptual position. For example first position is, understandably, the most common position. The perspectives involved with each of these positions are simply perceiving habits. With them come habits of thought. The great news is that they can be changed and expanded with skill-building exercises.

The difference in the quality of the three perspectives is significant. First position obviously contains more information about the feelings we have associated with the event. You will have access to information about physical sensations, feelings, and even smells and tastes. If the event was positive, then first position enables us to access the positive feelings related to it. However if the event was negative, maybe first position is not the best place from which to process it. After all who wants to make themselves feel bad?

Choosing How to See

I ran a stress management clinic for almost ten years in Northern Ireland. Many clients would explain that events in their past were making them feel depressed, scared, or sick. When I asked them a few questions about how they thought about those events, I discovered that most of the time the client was re-living the events and running them in their mind from first position. It was not surprising that they had to seek professional help. When I taught them the perceptual positions exercise, they discovered they had options in terms of from where they processed a memory (first, second or third position).

Asking our brain to change how it operates is a little like trying to write with our non-dominant hand. For most of us the process is messy at the start, but with practice it becomes easier. The pay-off for developing the ability to take different perspectives is an increased ability to understand a situation, to be able to look at it from two or three perspectives instead of just the same old one.

> *Asking our brain to change how it operates is like writing with our non-dominant hand.*

The exercise at the end of this chapter will help you learn how to use the three basic perspectives more systematically.

My mother used to tell me that an ounce of skill is better than a pound of knowledge. And knowing about the perspectives and not using them is a lot like knowing CPR but being unwilling to administer it — tragic.

When exploring the three perspectives, we begin to realize there are three truths.

1. We have a choice about which perspective we use to process a thought from the past, present or future.
2. Each perspective provides advantages and disadvantages.
3. Exploring all the perspectives better informs us about the event.

Leonardo de Vinci considered the first way he looked at a problem to be too biased towards his usual perspective. To overcome this bias he would look at the problem from one perspective, then another, and then another. With each change, he said, his understanding would grow. A closer examination of de Vinci's anatomical diagrams provides ample evidence that he never drew something from just one perspective. The effect of adding understanding by systematically using different perspectives may be why the different perspectives have been called "the three keys to wisdom". Even a blind man having taken the time to explore an elephant from many perspectives is much closer to wisdom than someone vigorously clutching just one part.

5. Frames — We've All Been Framed

Frames refer to the set of interpretations we choose to surround a particular event. If someone were to offer me a mint I could frame this gesture as an act of genuine friendliness and generosity. I could also frame it as a subtle way to suggest that I had bad breath. In most circumstances social etiquette prevents us from asking what the offer of the mint implied. We are left to perceive the event in a way that fits with our overall understanding of the situation. Our perceptions will determine how we operate in the situation as well. We could ask ourselves a useful question: "In what way can I choose to perceive this situation that will further enhance collaboration?" By answering this question we are developing our CQ.

Everyone has experienced interpreting someone's behavior in one way, only to find out later that their perception had been flawed. If reality is such an undependable construct, should we not just choose the frame that best allows us to be the most resilient? In other words, if we assume (use a frame) that a statement someone makes to us is well-intended, the frame has a particular effect. By framing their statement in a positive way we are indirectly creating a situation that is cooperative and friendly.

If, on the other hand, we frame someone's remarks as ill-intended, we will convey this in our tone of voice and body language. That may set the scene for a situation that is defensive and non-friendly. The actual intention of the other person is almost immaterial.

We cannot control other people, as much as we would like to think we can. The bottom line is that we can only be responsible for how *we* feel. So frames can be exceptionally useful when we wish to change the way *we* feel about something such as a memory or another person's behavior. Changing the frame we use is called "reframing" and, along with perceptual positions, is another one of the tools that enables us to be more resilient. The secret is to choose a frame that enables us to respond most resourcefully. The end result is that we are able to take control of a situation rather than allow it to control us.

Let's look at an example. Greg has discovered his boss, Jeff, has plans to ask him to work the weekend. He presupposes that this is because, of all the people that work in his department, Jeff likes Greg the least. This assumption leaves Greg feeling resentful toward Jeff and anxious about how he will be able to say "no" to the request. An alternative perspective Greg could take is that Jeff has chosen to delegate the work to him because he is the most skilled and reliable person. This set of assumptions (making up a frame) leaves Greg feeling valued and honored to be asked. Whether he really wants to work the weekend is immaterial at present. What is most affected will be the interaction between himself and his boss. Whether Greg says yes or no does not really matter. The overall outcome was reframed by Greg. He could have displayed feelings of resentment and put Jeff on the defensive. Either way Jeff will either feel more comfortable with his refusal, or will have begun to appreciate Greg more for saying yes. By reframing the situation Greg did not have to lie to himself or pretend things that were untrue. What he did was change the frame he used long enough to see how the situation played out. In this situation the CQ of both parties probably rose simply from choosing a different frame.

Any event or situation can be a good thing or a bad thing depending on how it is perceived. Highly resilient people have perceptual flexibility, enabling them to choose how they view a set of circumstances.

Often they will reframe a situation several times to enable them to maintain a sense of autonomy or control. This is called multiple reframing. A great example of this process is found in the Zen tradition.

THE FARMER AND HIS STALLION

There is an old Zen story about a farmer who bought a fine stallion one Monday at market for a good price. His neighbors came to admire it and all said "How fortunate you are!" To which the farmer replied
"Maybe..."

On the Tuesday the stallion escaped through a gap in the fence and ran away to the hills. Now all the neighbors said "How awful — what a catastrophe." To which the farmer replied
"Maybe..."

Then on Wednesday the stallion returned to the farm with a small herd of wild mares behind him. This time the neighbors were ecstatic — crying, "What luck! How marvelous."
To which the farmer replied
"Maybe..."

On the Thursday the farmer's only son was breaking in the wild mares when one of them threw him and

he broke his leg. In the evening the neighbors talked
of "the tragedy and misfortune."
To which the farmer replied
"Maybe..."

On Friday the Emperor's army came looking for able
bodied recruits to fight and almost certainly die in a
War in the North...the villagers said to the farmer —
"how fortunate for your son", the farmer replied...

The principle behind this story is that perception is a highly relative process. Maturana, the Chilean biologist, suggests that when we forget our relative view of reality, we lose our capacity to live together. He goes on to state that when one person or group insists that only they see "what is really going on", they are actually making a "demand for obedience". There are many examples of this process going on in the world today. Indeed most, if not all, international conflicts are caused by groups of people being certain about their own version of reality.

The demand for obedience worked successfully throughout the industrial era with organizations built upon power hierarchies. Now that we are entering the era of collective intelligence, where cooperation and CQ are premium skills, such demands are less effective and often very harmful to a team's overall resilience.

Emotional Perceptions

We're not passive observers of an external world;
rather, we know our world through interacting
with it, and our emotions can limit or enrich that
interaction.
HUMBERTO R. MATURANA

Maturana's observation leads us to the following question: "How are we choosing to interact with the world?" By looking for the bad or negative influences, we discover a limited and one-dimensional world. This emphasizes the power of perspective in building the CQ of groups and teams to which we belong.

> *Neuroscientists have discovered strong evidence that human intelligence, human memory, and human decisions are never completely rational but are always colored by emotions, as we all know from experience.*
> CAPRA, *THE WEB OF LIFE*

One factor that cannot be ignored is the part our emotions play in our perceptions. In fact research in this area demonstrates a connection between our success and general sense of happiness.

> *After interviewing 100 of the most successful and happy people they could find... The research found that each and every one of the 100 people had a special capability — to look for and find what is good in him- or herself, in others, and in all situations of life.*
> ENCYCLOPEDIA OF POSITIVE QUESTIONS

Emotions also play an important role in our level of self-mastery. The wisdom of this chapter can be encapsulated by the "Four Noble Truths" found in Buddhist philosophy.

- We all experience suffering in one way or another — mental, physical, emotional, spiritual.
- We create our own suffering. It is a consequence of our desiring things to be other than what they are.

- It need not be this way. We have a choice as to how we perceive the world and live our lives.
- There are systematic ways to go about changing how we think and perceive.

There are many ways to change how we think and perceive. The methods offered at the end of this chapter have been very success-ful with tens of thousands of people. Of course, nothing will change unless you are willing to try them.

Mirror, Mirror on the Wall

How we perceive ourselves determines how we operate in this world. Our self-perception is part of our relationship with ourselves. The relationship we have with ourselves is the most fundamental and abiding relationship we will ever have. If we are highly judgmen-tal with ourselves it will almost certainly be translated into a habit of being judgmental with others. The place where change starts is the self and nowhere is it more true than our perception of ourselves.

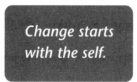

Change starts with the self.

> *When I view myself as a time-sensitive product,*
> *valued for what I produce, then I have made*
> *depth, extended thought, and the inward journey*
> *marginal indulgences. Instead of doing what matters,*
> *I spend my life doing what works. It increases*
> *my market value and postpones the question of my*
> *human value.*
> BLOCK, *THE ANSWER TO HOW IS YES*

The quote from Peter Block's book, *The Answer To How Is Yes*, defines the challenge we all face in a rapidly changing society. What is our human value? Does my personal journey have any impact upon my professional development? Without developing ourself as a human being (rather than a human "doing") we will fail to grow professionally in a sustainable fashion. Along with this is the task of developing our CQ, our capacity to tap into the energy of groups and networks, supporting others as they strive to achieve their outcomes and achieving our own, in the process.

 ## WHERE WE'VE BEEN

So we've explored the topic of perception in connection with resilience and the development of CQ. From this chapter we learned that:

- Perceptions are relative and become habits of seeing;
- Our attention is an important asset and used carefully can strengthen resilience and raise CQ;
- We use filters to select what we attend to and what we ignore;
- We can change the way we operate with others by changing our filters;
- Perspectives are ways of looking at things and we need to practice using different perspectives to increase our perceptual flexibility; and
- Frames are ways we interpret perceptions and reframing can help us respond more resourcefully to challenges.

WHERE WE'RE GOING

Biographies and autobiographies of great people point clearly to a distinct connection between how they saw the world and how they behaved in it. In this chapter we explored one half of the equation. In the next, we explore the other half — self-mastery. We will also examine ways to expand our own self-mastery and the part that can play in developing resilience and raising CQ.

CQ Tool© 2

Developing Perceptual Flexibility

This exercise achieves a number of things. It enables participants to discover for themselves specific processing capacities
of the mind. The realization that participants have a choice over
which processing capacity they use to review past events and
plan future ones.

STEP ONE: Close your eyes and think of a pleasant holiday
you have experienced. Notice the pictures/images as you recall
this event.

Note: There are two different perspectives from which you
can run your memories. One is where you are watching yourself in the memory (fly on the wall). This is called the Director's
Perspective. The other is when you are actually in the picture seeing things with your own eyes. This is the Actor's
Perspective.

Director's Perspective: When you are running a memory
from the director's perspective, you are taking a dissociated
position. You are seeing and hearing things from a position
removed from the scene. Typically, when you run memories
from this position, your feelings about this memory tend to
be diminished or absent altogether.

Actor's Perspective: When you are running a memory from the actor's perspective, the memory is running as if you were re-living the event within your own body. You do not see yourself in the pictures. Typically, you will have a heightened awareness of the feelings associated with that memory.

STEP TWO A: Notice the image you created. Are you in director's perspective where you see yourself in the picture? (If you cannot, then go to Step 2B.) In this case, to explore the actor's perspective, imagine stepping into your body in the event. Notice what it is like to be inside your own body. To help, you may like to imagine things like warmth or coolness or feelings of relaxation, etc.

STEP TWO B: Notice the image you created. Can you see things and hear things as if you were there? If so, you are running the memory from actor's perspective. In this case, imagine stepping out of your body and notice what it is like to be watching yourself in the event. You may notice the lessening of the feelings associated with this memory.

Note: Now you have had an opportunity to switch perspectives from where you normally run that memory. The advantage of being able to switch perspectives is that you can choose to have more or less feelings associated with the event.

STEP THREE: Practice switching from one perspective to the other. Doing this expands your perceptual flexibility. Try the exercise with other events. Notice by switching to the director's perspective, challenging or upsetting events become much more comfortable. They lack most (if not all) of the negative feelings that accompanied them originally. Likewise, if you had been running pleasant memories from the director's perspective, you will discover the memory has many more pleasant feelings to be enjoyed by switching to the actor's perspective.

Self-Mastery

Socrates demonstrated long ago, that the truly free individual is free only to the extent of his own self-mastery. While those who will not govern themselves are condemned to find masters govern over them.

STEVEN PRESSFIELD, *THE WAR OF ART*

In chapter 2, we explored the part perception plays in our resilience and in building resilient teams. Perception also plays a central role in our ability to develop self-mastery. In this chapter, we will explore how to develop greater self-mastery and how developing it will affect the creation of resilient teams. We will also examine the connection between self-mastery and further enhancing our CQ.

The First Furrow

When I was ten years old my mom sent me with tea and biscuits down to the fields where my father was plowing. When I got there, he had just started a new field and was half-way down the first furrow. I decided to wait until he came back up the field. He took ages — every now and again getting off the tractor to tap something, or adjust part of the plow. By the time he returned to my end of the field I had begun to wonder just how long it was going to take him to plow the whole field. "Dad," I said, "I have watched you plowing the first furrow and if it takes you as long to plough every furrow, it's going to take you all day to plough this little field."

"Well son that was the first furrow of the field — it's the most important, because it sets the pattern for the rest of the field." He went on to tell me that when it came time for me to plow a field and if I found I didn't like the pattern when I had finished, I should check the first furrow and I would usually find that the problem started there.

> *In reading the lives of great men, I found that*
> *the first victory they won was over themselves...*
> *self-discipline with all of them came first.*
> HARRY S. TRUMAN

On reflection, I realize my dad was sharing a valuable insight. So often we become aware of patterns in our lives that we don't like. Sometimes we even try to fix the pattern — the one that's "out there" somewhere — when really the first furrow is where the pattern is set, within ourselves. In human relations (and communication) the human heart is where the first furrow is cut. How we relate to ourselves sets the tone and the shape of the cut line for the ones to follow. It is easier to look outside ourselves than look inside. Often an ounce of change made within easily outweighs a pound of change made without.

The first furrow connects personal development (the responsibility to develop ourselves) to professional development. To pretend that they do not affect each other is naive. A company may wish to hire the person's skills, but inevitably they end up with the person's attitudes in the bargain.

> *An ounce of change made within easily outweighs a pound of change made without.*

> *Sustained great results depend upon building a culture full of self disciplined people who take disciplined action, fanatically.*
>
> *A culture of discipline is not just about action. It is about getting disciplined people who engage in disciplined thought and who then take disciplined action.*
>
> COLLINS, *GOOD TO GREAT*

The metaphor of the first furrow emphasizes the responsibility we each have for our own behavior and how much this behavior depends upon the relationship we have with ourselves. Building greater trust with others is one thing, building greater trust in ourselves is another. Close examination of resilient teams uncovers that they are made up of individuals with great levels of self-mastery. Not only does this ensure that everyone pulls their weight, it also means that each member is a good role model for the rest of the team. High levels of self-mastery are also associated with people who have high CQs, in that they actively pursue collaboration with others.

The most obvious question is, "How do we develop greater self-mastery?" First let us look at what are the most important skills that make up self-mastery.

1. Perceptual Flexibility
2. Making Meaning
3. Emotional Management
4. Mental Models
5. Leadership and Followship
6. Intention
7. Persistence
8. Alignment
9. Self-Expression

In the following pages we will discover how each plays their part in building self-mastery and how to strengthen our own sense of it. The truth is we *already* have a great deal of self-mastery at work in our lives. It is made up of a composite of the nine elements mentioned above. Consciously making improvements — even small ones — in these nine areas will enable us to deepen our self-mastery.

1. Perceptual Flexibility

In chapter 2 we explored how we can use multiple perspectives to enable us to *choose* how we looked at things. Choosing how to see something is exercising **perceptual flexibility**. Individuals with high levels of self-mastery choose how they look at things in order to deal with them more effectively.

> *No occurrences are so unfortunate that the*
> *shrewd cannot turn them to some advantage, nor*
> *so fortunate that the imprudent cannot turn them*
> *to their own disadvantage.*
> DUC DE LA ROCHEFOUCAULD

Perceptual strategies are evident in the way people approach life. Highly resilient people display strong optimistic strategies.

This may not be exhibited as the classic "rose-tinted glasses", rather it is demonstrated as a deliberately chosen, *useful* perspective. Within resilient people this manifests as the ability to turn practically everything that happens to some advantage.

Here are some of the features that distinguish optimistic strategies from pessimistic ones.

When something pleasant happens to someone using a pessimistic perspective, they:

- credit luck;
- predict it can't last; or
- localize the effect.

When something challenging happens, they:

- blame themselves;
- generalize to other areas of life; or
- predict the future based on their present conditions.

We have all used these strategies from time to time in our lives. However, it is obvious that if we were to apply them to everything, the consequences would be pretty tragic.

On the other hand when something pleasant happens to someone taking an optimistic perspective, they:

- take some credit for the effect;
- look for a positive trend; or
- generalize the effect.

When something challenging happens, they:

- remember that there is no failure, only feedback;
- take it as an exception to the rule; or
- consider it as an isolated incident.

The same incident, challenging or pleasant, is treated quite differently by the two types of strategies. The next time something happens to you that could be considered unpleasant or pleasant, stop and consider what strategies you are applying. Strategies are like habits of thought and, as such, old ways of dealing with things will be the first to impose their will. We only have to stop and ask the question "How else could I approach this?" to begin the process of breaking free of our old habits.

Foul Ball or Strike?

People with high levels of self-mastery have the ability to create useful meanings for events in their lives. The story of the three umpires illustrates this point.

Three umpires are discussing how they approach umpiring. The youngest among them explains that he "calls them as they are". The next umpire states that he "calls them as he sees them". The oldest and craftiest of them says that "they are as I call them". The old umpire realized that he was able to define the game by choosing how to see the play. In effect he is *choosing the meaning of what he sees* and he knows it.

Scientific evidence suggests that the strategy of perceptual flexibility provides benefits that go beyond the psychological. In a study authored by Christopher Peterson of the University of Michigan (*Journal of Personality and Social Psychology*, 1989, p. 55), it was shown that there appears to be a direct link between illness and pessimism. The study examined how subjects viewed events in their lives. Following the test group over a 35-year period, the study showed that subjects with negative interpretations were consistently sicker than their more optimistic peers. These kinds of findings have been replicated many times since. It is not surprising to find that psychonueroimmunology (the study of how the mind affects the body) is one of the fastest growing areas of research in medicine.

Because resilience not only relates to our minds but also to our bodies, one strongly impacts the other. I know several people who do all the right things for their body — vitamins, good nutrition and regular exercise — but unfortunately they harbor negative emotions and beliefs about their health. Their thought patterns may be negating much of the positive physical care by suppressing their immune system. If we can make ourselves sick or well with our thoughts, we can certainly make ourselves less or more resilient with them.

GO DEEPER

Mind Body Connection: www.anthillsite.com

2. Making Meaning

A Native American elder once described
his own inner struggles in this manner:
Inside of me there are two dogs.
One of the dogs is mean and evil.
The other dog is good.
The mean dog fights the good dog all the time.
When asked which dog wins,
he reflected for a moment and replied,
The one I feed the most.
GEORGE BERNARD SHAW

Viktor Frankl's *Man's Search for Meaning* and *The Unheard Cry For Meaning* were written as testaments to this deceivingly simple idea — we *are* the meaning makers. During the Second World War he was held in several different concentration camps. His experience there brought him to the realization that all his "freedoms" had been taken from him, except the freedom to choose what the experience *meant*. This insight probably saved Frankl's life and those people who embraced his approach. In Frankl's own words, "the sort of person the prisoner became was the result of an inner decision" and that decision centered on creating a meaning for himself. By changing the meaning he could change the way he responded to the horrible conditions in which he found himself. This led his captors to change the way they treated him and the other prisoners who participated in this strategy. The result was that Frankl was able to wrench something of great value from very dire circumstances. Upon his release at the end of the war, this series of insights led him to develop a new psychotherapy, called Logotherapy, which has had a significant impact on clinical practice. The central tenet to this form of therapy is that no matter what happens to you, you always have the freedom to choose what it means to you.

Choose a meaning that makes you feel more resourceful and resilient.

> *To an ordinary man everything is either a curse or a blessing, but to a Man of Knowledge everything is a challenge and an opportunity.*
> TEACHINGS OF DON JUAN

Just as you can choose from what perspective to look at something, you can also *choose a meaning* that makes you feel more resourceful and resilient.

GO DEEPER

Making Meaning: www.anthillsite.com

3. Emotional Self-Management

Most of the time we manage our emotions quite unconsciously. The importance of emotional self-mastery has been firmly established through the work of Daniel Goleman and his concept of Emotional Intelligence (EQ). When faced with challenging situations and challenging people, expressing EQ obviously becomes more valuable. However, emotional self-mastery is just as important during times of high performance.

GO DEEPER

Emotional Intelligence: www.anthillsite.com

> *You don't drown by falling in the water;*
> *you drown by staying there.*
> EDWIN LOUIS COLE

Mastery over emotions is a central element of highly resilient people. Our emotions provide us with the power to act and are an important source of self-nurturance. Fear is the most common problematic emotion. Many successful athletes report how they managed to turn their fear into a source of energy enabling them to achieve great accomplishments. (The exercise at the end of chapter 2 (Perception) can also be used to harness your emotions.) Our emotional response to a situation is directly related to how we perceive it. The feeling of excitement when taking a seat in a roller coaster is biochemically identical to the feeling we have before we sit down in the dentist's chair. What differs is how we perceive the two events and consequently how we interpret the feelings. In other words if we wish to change the way we are responding to a situation, we can change the way we look at it.

Emotional self-management is also closely related to self-esteem. Nathaniel Branden has described self-esteem as "the reputation we have acquired with ourselves". He goes on to say that "There is no value-judgment more important to man — no factor more decisive in his psychological development and motivation — than the estimate he passes on himself."

⬇ GO DEEPER
Self-Esteem Survey: www.anthillsite.com

4. Mental Models

The fourth aspect of self-mastery is *mental models*. These are deeply rooted assumptions and ways of thinking that guide the way we think about the world. They are described as mental because they exist in our minds and models because they are constructs created as a result of our own experience of life. They are often used as maps to navigate our future experiences. Everyone has them and, like the Zen fish, in chapter 1, we don't notice them most of the time. One thing is certain — they are ours and they affect the way we respond to our world.

In the practice of *systems thinking*, changing mental models is considered to be the only way to eliminate a problem, rather than just solve it. When we *solve* a problem it may reappear again. When we *eliminate* it, that particular problem will never reappear (don't worry there are plenty others) because we have changed our mental models with respect to the issue. Mental models are created out of beliefs and based on our assumptions (chapter 1).

The reason we explore this topic here rather than under assumptions (chapter 1) is that mental models are more than just beliefs and they have such a profound impact. The secret to improving self-mastery through mental models is to develop systematic ones. Deliberately chosen mental models will help achieve the objectives we set.

In their book *The Art of Systems Thinking*, Joseph O'Connor and Ian McDermott suggest following simple rules to enable you to have more systemic mental models.

- Admit your mental models are your best guess at the moment and be on the lookout for better ones.
- Have wide interests
- Be comfortable with ambiguity.
- Be curious about, and pay particular attention to, experiences that seem to contradict your mental models.
- Have a wide time horizon to look for feedback.
- When confronted with a problem, look at the assumptions you are making about the situation as well as the situation itself.
- Look for relationships, how events fit together.
- Look for loops and circles of cause and effect, the effect of one cause being the cause of another effect.

Choosing our mental models is the mark of highly resilient and successful professionals. The concept of CQ is a mental model. As a result of adopting it we begin to look for ways to increase collaboration and actively seek ways of building stronger relationships. The "assumption-busting" strategy explored in chapter 1 is particularly good at altering mental models. Too often we wander around the world without checking the filters we use to process events and relationships in our lives.

5. Leadership and Followship

Leading and following are two behaviors that have created the greatest number of theories and books in relation to business. For a group of individuals to function together some leading has to be going on and some following. That's the simple part over. Traditional models of command and control involve a distinct hierarchy of command. Orders are issued from the top and fed down through the hierarchy to the lowest levels. Since the dawn of the industrial revolution this system has been considered to be the only way people could be organized around work.

The *mechanistic view* inherited from Newton's model of the universe probably encouraged this view of how people work. The mechanistic view also implied that the lowest levels of the organization had the least knowledge and was in the worst position from which to make decisions. Managers at the top were considered to be in a better position because they had the "big picture", enabling them to make executive decisions that became a set of directions to the lower ranks. In such a system, the personal initiative required from people at the front line was generally very low. We are still occasionally told "I'll have to ask the manager", indicating the person has not been granted the decision-making power necessary.

The command and control method of management and business innovation is proving too cumbersome for forward-thinking companies. Many are discovering the advantages of using "bottom–up" intelligence. This perspective takes the view that people at the front line are in a better position to make decisions because they are closest to the changing environment. More enlightened companies are realizing that to survive they are going to have to become much more adaptive to the changes occurring in the market. The bottom-up model (which we explore in greater detail in chapter 5) also requires team members to have adequate levels of self-mastery. Without it they will not be able to exercise their initiative when required.

Bottom-up processing makes it possible for companies to increase speed and effectiveness of service by enabling the front-line staff to deal with practically anything they encounter. More and more companies are realizing the advantages of allowing front-line staff to have the power to make more decisions. It enables the company to flatten their own structure, making do with less middle management. Another outcome of bottom-up processing is that high levels of self-reliance are required of everyone in the company. This in turn places more emphasis on all the team members' levels of self-mastery.

Yin and Yang

> *In a truly self-organizing system, the part of the team that is in the best position to act and has the greatest amount of knowledge will lead.*

The concept of *followship* has been with us for a few years. It is defined here as the ability to follow and support the efforts of a self-organizing team. In a truly self-organizing system, the part of the team that is in the best position to act and has the greatest amount of knowledge will lead. This means that within a resilient team leadership frequently flows through the membership depending on where they are in the process. As conditions change leadership may shift many times. During these transitions each individual needs to be able to shift from followship to leadership and back to followship as the situation demands. The skills involved in good followship are as outlined below.

- The ability to see what needs to be done and do it when it needs to be done.

- Flexibility in behaviors to support fellow team members as they shift from follower to leader.
- An awareness of the team as a *functioning whole* where each individual is willing to lead and to follow as circumstances dictate.
- A capacity to build collaborative relationships that support the team and the individuals that make it up.

These skills could also be considered as core in the development of our CQ and the CQ of any team to which we belong.

6. Intention

Intention is one of our most valuable assets. It has a huge impact in the area of setting outcomes. In other words, how our intention has been set has a significant effect on how likely it is that we will achieve our outcomes. For example, setting the intention to build collaborative relationships will automatically make it much more likely that such relationships will be created.

Properly formed intention enables the creation of a *well formed outcome*. Resilient individuals with high levels of self-mastery frequently achieve their outcomes. Laurence Boldt said, "You wouldn't think of building a new home without a blueprint. Yet many of us try to live our lives without a clear sense of the results we are after." There are probably many people reading this book right now who have extensive plans and objectives for their next vacation, but have given no such attention to what they wish to achieve with their team.

The benefits of a well formed outcome are the following:

- We *notice* what is useful for our objective.
- We *remember* what is useful to our objective.

- Our objective determines our *selection of perceptions*.
- Our objective *affects our thought* patterns.
- Our thoughts and perceptions can help us *reach our objectives*.

Of course the more clearly defined our outcomes/objectives are, the more likely it will be that the benefits will materialize.

There are two types of objectives — away-from and towards. An away-from, sometimes known as the problem-focused objective, motivates us to solve the problem or achieve the objective by getting *away from* something or reducing something.

A department trying to reduce absenteeism is a good example of an activity which is away-from. Certain strategies and policies are implemented to *get away* from high levels of employee absences. The other side of the coin is how the department could be run to move *towards* high levels of employee engagement. Strategies designed to create a workplace that people love to come to will also have the effect of lowering absenteeism. In this example the objective was basically the same but the *intention* formed was quite different. The question has changed from "what do we want less of" to "what do we want more of". In that switch, what has changed is the perspective taken and the strategy adopted. Towards strategies are also known as solution-focused.

Robert Fritz, in his book *The Path of Least Resistance*, explains that away-from outcomes are poorly designed because they do not take into account how human beings are motivated. In the case of away-from outcomes, as he sees it, each time a portion of the objective is achieved, the less motivation there is to continue, like a moth flying away from the light because of the heat. At some point the heat diminishes and causes the moth's attraction for the light to once again override. Thus the moth is caught in limbo until it collapses of exhaustion.

Many organizational challenges exist only because they have been phrased and approached in an away-from manner. In other words they were not designed for success; they were designed to avoid failure. For example a company focused on getting out of debt may end up using different strategies to achieve that objective, than a company that plans to maximize revenue. Reducing debt is, after all, only half the story. The pressure to reduce debt will ease as the debt falls, therefore progress slows and it takes longer to achieve the outcome. All companies want to make a profit and a towards objective (such as maximizing profits) creates more of the desired result as it gains its objectives.

A salesperson with the target of selling 50 cars each month is motivated by the number *sold* that increases as the month passes. Notice that they are not motivated by the number they still have to sell, although some people choose to motivate themselves that way. Neither of these approaches is good or bad.

Fritz's comprehensive research in this area clearly shows that most successful people are motivated by things they were building rather than things they were tearing down (except demolition experts of course). Fritz uses the term "creative tension" to describe the process of connecting a desired goal to the present reality. Imagine an elastic band stretched between two points. The very act of connecting them with an elastic band will make it more likely that the two will be drawn together. Also

> *Successful people are motivated by things they were building rather than things they were tearing down.*

being drawn towards something (e.g., profit) is much more motivating for most of us than being pushed away from something (e.g., debt). This is one of the main reasons why the concept of creative tension and well formed outcomes are more successful than away-from strategies.

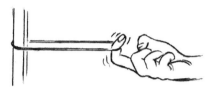

Addressing the South African people, Nelson Mandela spoke much more about creating a rainbow nation than he did about taking down the apartheid system. Intuitively he knew that if they had focused on taking it down, at the end of the process all they would have left was a large and dangerous political hole. So instead he focused their energy on the creative tension existing between where they were as a fledgling nation and where they wished to end up. The result was the rainbow coalition that amazed the world by creating a largely peaceful transition.

All well and good, but we live in a complex world where objectives and outcomes are not always of our making. Many times they are handed to us or to our team. The argument here is that no matter in what form they are presented, we can choose to apply a towards or away-from strategy to them. (For a method of creating well formed outcomes, see the exercise at the end of this chapter.) The solution-focused approach, builds beautifully into the strength-based/appreciative approach as both emphasize that we "find what we look for".

Using intention is also called "beginning with the end in mind". It can be explained best with the story of the young soldier. A young soldier is found in the barracks by his captain. He is pulling all the bunks apart, emptying all the cupboards, pulling up the rugs and making a horrible mess. The Captain says, "Son, what are you doing?" The young soldier says, "I'm looking for a piece of paper." He says,

"Well, you're making a mess and you better stop it or I'll put you on a charge." The soldier totally ignores him and continues tearing the barracks apart. Eventually the Captain says, "Look, son, that's the last time I'm going to warn you." But still it goes on. So he calls the military police and they whip him down to the brig to let him cool off for a while.

He's only in the cell for a few moments when the jailor hears a commotion in the cell. There is the soldier moving anything that isn't bolted down. The jailor shouts in through the door, "What are you doing, Private?" The soldier says, "I'm looking for a piece of paper." The jailor says, "Well there's no piece of paper in there, buddy. You just stop making such a fuss." The young soldier ignores him and continues to ransack the cell.

The jailor decides to call up the army psychiatrist. "We've got a real cookie down here Doc, you gotta see this guy. He's something else." The psychiatrist says, "Well, send him up." The MPs bring him up to the psychiatrist's office. The young solider is only in the office a few seconds when he starts pulling everything apart. The psychiatrist asks him what he is doing. The soldier says, "Looking for a piece of paper." A few sessions later, the same scene playing out each time, the psychiatrist becomes exasperated and says, "Look Private, I have decided after much reflection that you are not cut out for the army, and the army is not cut out for you. I am signing your dismissal." He hands the young soldier the dismissal form and the young man says, "There's the piece of paper I was looking for."

Reflect on this for a moment. What if the captain asked the soldier, "What are you doing?" and this young soldier said, "I'm trying to get out of the army." Do you think he would have been discharged? I don't think so either. In this story the intention the young soldier had set enabled him to navigate the Captain, the jailor and the army psychiatrist. He remained focused on what he wanted (the piece of paper) rather than what he did not want (to be in the army any longer).

Using Our Signal Lights

One final thought around the topic of intention is the need for us to broadcast our intention. Once you have developed a well formed outcome, you must find ways to broadcast it and then be sensitive to your environment as it responds to that announcement. On the highway, for instance, we switch on our signal lights to let other drivers know we wish to change lanes. So it is with life: if we wish to change lanes we should allow others to know of our intention. Think of the number of times when you set an intention and suddenly resources became available to you that you didn't know existed. This had more to do with you broadcasting your intention than it had to do with miracles.

Designing outcomes and setting our attention implies we are willing to take personal responsibility for ourselves and our behaviors. This is another important element of the self-mastery underlying the resilient individual. Setting positive intention is also about a central part of further enhancing our collaborative intelligence. By actively seeking positive outcomes with others, we are raising our CQ at the same time.

Viktor Frankl once said that the United States should have built a statue of responsibility on the west coast to balance the Statue of Liberty on the east coast. What he was getting at was that we all wish to have more liberty or freedom and not necessarily any of the responsibility that comes with that freedom. For instance the freedom to drive on the public highways is matched by the responsibility to drive in a safe and courteous manner.

7. Persistence

Nothing in the world can take the place of persistence.

Talent will not;
nothing is more common than unsuccessful men
with talent.

Genius will not;
unrewarded genius is almost a proverb.

Education will not;
the world is full of educated derelicts.

Persistence and determination alone are omnipotent.

ELEANOR ROOSEVELT

There are two sides to every story. Persistence can be associated with stubbornness. Winston Churchill's call to "never give in" can be used by the frog as an excuse to stay in the pan while it simply boils to death. Therefore I think an important element of persistence is the use of judgment in choosing what to hold onto and what to let go off. Another story may help to clarify.

> A great deal of success in life is based upon knowing what to hold onto and what to let go off.

Two monks are walking along a path. They come to a river and meet a pretty young girl, just standing there wondering how she is going to get across. One of the monks offers to carry the girl over the river. After they had all crossed and the monks had been walking for some time along the path on their own once again, the monk who had watched his companion help the girl said, "Brother I have been thinking for some time about this and we both know that our order forbids us to have contact with the opposite sex. Are you not concerned for your soul?" The other monk said, "Are you still carrying her? I set her down two miles ago."

One of the monks in this story knew just how long he needed to hold onto the young girl, the other didn't. The country and western singer Kenny Rogers would have described it as "knowing when to hold em and when to fold em". In other words there is a fine line between persistence and stubborn stupidity.

Sometimes hindsight is the only thing that will tell us the difference. And sometimes if we hold on for long enough fate steps in. When I was a young child living on an isolated farm, the summers were often long and lonely. I lived a considerable distance from my nearest friend. After working in the fields with my father all day I often amused myself by exploring a set of old buildings belonging to a neighbor. One evening I discovered a small hole in a stone wall supporting an old cowshed. Lying near it on the ground was a metal stake, the type they used to fasten the roof. I began to chisel a stone out of the wall with the spike. This became a favorite pastime of mine during the summer. I would make my way over to the shed in the evening and knock out another stone.

Weeks later, toward the end of summer, there had been a storm with strong winds. My older brother, Pierce, came into the house at supper time and said, "You've knocked Billy Greer's cowshed down." No one at the kitchen table knew what he was talking about — except me of course. I didn't know what to say, and eventually got into a great deal of trouble with my parents over the incident. The hole I had created, one small stone at a time, had so weakened the building that a gust of wind came along and finished the job. The lesson I took from this experience was that you don't always have to finish the job yourself — beginning it and working steadily will allow other factors to play a part — sometimes with spectacular results. In this case my persistence generated a good thrashing from my father, but on the other hand persistence can generate good things too.

Dr. Robert Ornstein has conducted a great deal of research in the area of how people use their brains. His research shows that when we use both sides of our brains (there is a natural tendency for people to use one side predominately), we greatly increase our functional capacity. Some subjects increased their performance by a factor of ten (X10) when they used both sides of their brain. Brain Gym™, stemming from the intensive research of Dr. Paul and Gail E. Dennison, provides a series of simple exercises designed to balance the use of the two sides of the brain.

GO DEEPER
Brain Gym: www.anthillsite.com

Persistence is difficult to maintain if we do not manage our energy properly. We have a finite amount to expend and how we focus it depends entirely on how we align ourselves.

8. Alignment

Self-mastery relies on our ability to focus *and*, in turn, upon our ability to create *alignment*. Alignment enables us to have the greatest impact in our lives. Robert Dilts created a model that describes our lives as consisting of a series of levels. He called these the "logical level" and they are:

- environment,
- behaviors,
- capabilities,

- beliefs,
- values,
- identity and
- spirit.

Arranged as a series of concentric circles (see Figure 3.1), the levels represent different aspects of our lives.

Figure 3.1
Dilts' Logical Levels

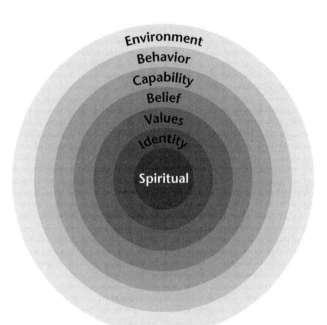

- **Environment.** At the outer level, we have our physical environment: material possessions, our homes, and the people in our lives. This is the part of our life that is most visible to ourselves and to others. The environment also contains all our relationships. We have accumulated all these things (good or bad) from the new level — our behaviors.

- **Behaviors.** This level includes everything we do in our personal and professional lives. Our behaviors, to a large extent, have created our environment. If we wish to change our environment we must change our behaviors. Our behaviors are largely dependent upon our capabilities.
- **Capabilities.** This refers to all the things of which we are capable. Not all capabilities become expressed as behaviors. For example I might be capable of driving my car at 150 MPH. I don't allow that to become a behavior because I do not like the anticipated consequences for myself or other drivers. Capabilities are potential behaviors, some become actualized and others don't. The difference between those that turn into behaviors and those that don't is whether there is support at the belief level.
- **Beliefs.** These store all the things we assume about ourselves, others, and the world in which we live. Beliefs are about permission. They give it or take it away, depending on how they are structured. Often enough we wish to be capable of something and when we think about it carefully we find we do not have sufficient belief in ourselves. We have not given ourselves permission. The beliefs we form rely heavily upon the things we value.
- **Values.** What we value will affect our relationship to the world. We focus our energy around those things that have the greatest value to us. We form strong assumptions and opinions around our values and, as such, they become the birthplace of most of our beliefs. In their own right they are the source of our motivation and therefore become very important when we are trying to achieve something. If we do not have a belief about something, it is unlikely that we will generate any capabilities or behaviors related to it. As you can see, each level depends on the content of the one below.

- **Identity.** Who are we? This can include our ethnic and cultural heritage (even if we don't associate ourselves with it any longer). Roles such as father, teacher, and artist often have a significant affect at this level. How we perceive ourselves (our identity) determines what we value.

- **Spirit.** The core of the model represents our spirit. Spirit need not be interpreted in any religious fashion. I think of spirit as the deepest level of us that knows it is alive in an alive universe. At this level it is common for people to be aware of how deeply connected they are to everyone and everything. The condition of our spirit determines, to a great degree, our identity (and so on up the through the layers).

  When people refer to the "spirit of the team" this is the level that is expressing itself and probably the level at which the team has connected. Everyone has had an experience where they have felt this level of connection with other people. This is one of the reasons why people who have had spiritual experiences sometimes undergo dramatic changes in their: beliefs and values; identities; capabilities, and behaviors.

Alignment is the process of bringing the different levels into line with each other. This can be achieved individually and also between individuals in a group, say within a team. Typically changes made at any of the deeper levels will reverberate, like ripples over the surface of a pond, out to the environment level. In my experience using this model with individuals and teams, huge changes can occur at the surface (environment/behaviors) with just small adjustments at deeper levels.

Aligning our own logical levels is not as complex as you might imagine. One of the most common discoveries people make when they perform an alignment process is that even very negative and self-limiting behaviors are attempts to honor a positive value situated at a deeper level. For example, someone that is overly strict and dictatorial with a colleague who reports to him may find through alignment questions that this behavior is based on the value of helping the person get the best out of himself. This alignment process is featured in the companion workbook.

Team alignment can be used to help individuals align the logical levels together. Of course, good personal alignment is a necessary first step to good team alignment. Try making a neat bundle out of a set of very crooked twigs and you'll know what I mean. There are significant benefits of bringing about this degree of alignment. Many teams are designed more around compliance than commitment. We should remember that commitment is a much more powerful motivator. The real reason commitment is not more common within the corporate world is that most managers and team leaders do not have a systematic way to generate it within their teams. The logical levels alignment process can be invaluable in these circumstances.

Team alignment also requires us to be actively developing our CQ. High performing teams are aligned and exercise all their collaborative intelligence around their shared objectives.

9. Self-Expression

At the very beginning of this chapter I shared the story of the first furrow and it's relevance to how we operate in the world, particularly with others. The kind of relationship we have with ourselves affects the way we use *self-expression*. The kinds of things we say about ourselves lets others know what sort of opinion we have of ourselves. Even things we say about others reveal a great deal of information, indirectly stated, about how we think of ourselves. Being highly judgmental toward another team member probably indicates we are very judgmental with ourselves.

Negative messages we received during our childhood are often absorbed and replayed whenever we experience an event that challenges our self-esteem. What we say about ourselves affects how other people perceive us. Conversely positive messages we received during our childhood are absorbed and act as a supportive reference when we encounter challenges to our self-esteem.

The things we say are based upon how we feel about ourselves. If we discover that our references to ourselves are less than flattering, then maybe it is time to reassess on what our self-esteem is based.

When someone is being highly judgmental of us we can, at the least, try to avoid them. When we are doing the judging, getting out of the way is not really an option. Self-expression is important in another way. How we express ourselves affects how other people relate to us — as implied earlier in this chapter. If we have a critical and negative relationship with ourselves this stands a very good chance of being translated into critical, negative relationships with our colleagues. Such relationships cannot build resilient teams.

Communicating our positive regard and respect for the people on our team will help build a team with strong resilient relationships and further strengthen our own CQ and that of the team. The next chapter explores the skill of communication. We will also address a number of questions. How does our communication affect our CQ and that of the team in which we operate? How can we build strong teams that weather change and pull together no matter what?

 ## WHERE WE'VE BEEN

This chapter has been about self-mastery and the role it plays in developing resilience and raising CQ. The main points of this chapter are:

- Self-mastery begins with taking personal responsibility for where we are.

- Developing our perceptual flexibility expands our self-mastery.
- We are the meaning makers and we define our own reality by interpreting it.
- Emotional self-management is a central element of self-mastery.
- Mental models are useful ways to manage our beliefs and assumptions about life.
- Leadership and followship are two sides of the same coin and both are becoming increasingly important in the highly dynamic society in which we live.
- Intention is a potent force for developing self-mastery and in reaching our life objectives.
- Persistence can compensate for shortcomings in other areas and is an important aspect of self-mastery.
- Alignment of energy (e.g., beliefs, behaviors and values) serves to strengthen self-mastery and develop CQ within teams.

 ## WHERE WE'RE GOING

Self-mastery is primarily important to the individual. However very few people work in total isolation. The further development of self-mastery requires that we know how to positively influence others. To do this we must know how to communicate effectively. The next chapter explores the topic of using communication to strengthen resilience and build CQ within teams.

CQ Tool© 3

Self-Mastery and Eliciting a Well Formed Outcome

In this chapter we have explored one of the distinguishing features of someone with strong self-mastery, namely their ability to create well formed outcomes. The following is a series of questions which can be used to elicit a well formed outcome.

For this exercise think of something you would like to achieve. It is important that you choose something that you really want and that would make a difference to your life — that will ensure you engage meaningfully with the exercise and be motivated to follow through. Also as far as chunk size is concerned, world peace may be a little large (considering this may be the first time you have ever completed this exercise) and a new haircut may not have enough going for it to fully engage you. Somewhere in between will probably work best. Take your time to fully explore all the possible answers to the questions — the more specific you are, the more likely the process will work for you.

1. What do you want? (E.g., is anyone already doing what you want to do?)

   _____

   _____

   _____

   _____

   _____

2. What's stopping you?

_____

_____

_____

_____

_____

3. Where, When, with Whom?

_____

_____

_____

_____

_____

4. What resources can you use? People, personal things, and things you don't already have?

_____

_____

_____

_____

_____

5. Time, Money, Effort needed?

_____

_____

_____

_____

_____

6. What are the present benefits of the present situation? (What is the secondary gain?)

_____

_____

_____

_____

_____

_____

_____

_____

_____

Note: In relation to question 6 — present benefits — it is common for people to have the reaction, "But surely there are no benefits to the present situation." This is a natural response; however psychologists call these benefits secondary gains. Like the small child that continues to misbehave, knowing that he is likely to receive another slap from his parent, the secondary gain is the attention he receives and the form in which he receives it is less important. In other words the secondary gain will continue to reinforce the behavior until the child discovers another way to ensure he can get attention from the parent. Likewise with things in our lives that we may wish to change — even with things that on the surface provide no perceivable reward — there may well be a secondary gain. For example if someone were frequently avoiding promotion at work, the secondary gain may be that they will not have to make adjustments to the relationships they have established with their co-workers. Surfacing the secondary gain can be a powerful catalyst in moving forward with a desired outcome.

7. How will others be affected? (Explore second and third positions.)

_____

_____

_____

_____

_____

_____

_____

8. What are the consequences? What else might happen if you got this outcome?

_____

_____

_____

_____

_____

_____

9. What actions will you take? Are others involved? If so how can you build in value for them?

_____

_____

_____

_____

_____

_____

_____

10. Ecology: does the outcome feel right? Is there anything missing? Place yourself into the future having achieved this thing and then answer this question again. Is there a difference in your answers?

_____

_____

_____

_____

_____

_____

_____

11. What larger outcomes are supported?

_____

_____

_____

_____

_____

_____

_____

Communication

Communication is the essential medium of a creative culture: the communal sea in which we all swim. A company that can't communicate is like a jazz band without instruments: Music just isn't going to happen.

JOHN KAO

This chapter brings us to the topic of communication and connects the previous themes of assumption-building, perception-making and self-mastery. After all, great self-mastery can only achieve so much if we are working within a team that does not communicate effectively.

More specifically, we will look at the role dialogue plays and examine how questions can serve a vital function in professional and team settings.

Top Down — Bottoms Up

The word "communication" can have many meanings. In a business setting it can refer to persuasion, collaboration, issues management, public relations, or employee communication. Sadly, most business training programs do not cover these topics deeply enough. These skills are increasingly required to enable flattened organizations to operate.

We are now discovering that the top down, command and control management philosophy is giving way to the horizontally structured (flattened) company. In this environment good communication skills are essential to provide continuity and interaction across teams and departments. Communication is the single most important human skill and, like anything that is always there, it can easily become invisible. Yet communication is one of the central skills to building stronger CQ within teams and organizations.

William Isaacs, president of Dialogos, explains that, "The problems that even the most practical organizations have — in improving their performance and obtaining the results they desire — can be traced directly to their ability to think and talk together, particularly at critical times." Often treated as a soft skill, communication is the backbone of every organization and affects everything and everybody involved in that organization.

All personal and professional relationships are built on rapport. Rapport is defined as a relationship of mutual understanding or trust and agreement between people. It is also described as the process of getting "into sync" with another person. Effective communication cannot occur without it.

To expand and develop our communication skills we must first become aware of how we are exercising the skills we have right now. In this chapter we will explore skills that expand our ability to communicate effectively both one-to-one and in groups.

Manipulation or Influence?

Often when people think about learning how to influence others with their communication, they ask, "isn't that manipulation?" This is an important question. All communication is influence, everyone is influencing everyone else whether they mean to or not. The more relevant question is, "how do I wish to influence this person?" not "will I?" Most influence is directionless and without purpose. The moment we add direction and purpose it runs the risk of being labeled as manipulation.

Communication skills are a tool, like a scalpel, for example. A scalpel can be taken to a hospital and used to save someone's life. The same implement could be used to hold up a convenience store. The sharper the scalpel the more capable it is for either purpose. The most significant factor is the *intent* of the person holding the tool. Responsibility rests with the person using the skill, not with the skill itself. This is where the rubber hits the road — are we taking advantage of the other person? Or are we seeking to discover a win-win situation, where the other person gains from the situation more or less equally?

In chapter 1, we explored how the assumptions we hold about life are fundamental to how we operate in the world. In this chapter I am making a specific set of assumptions about communication. I am going to ask you to take on these assumptions and use them as you explore this book. When you have finished the book, only adopt those that work for you.

- **Rapport is meeting individuals in their map of the world.**
  Rapport is defined here as a relationship of mutual trust and respect. Rapport is established through matching the other person's body language and language patterns and by being willing to enter their world rather than inviting them to visit ours.

- **Communication is both verbal and non-verbal, both conscious and unconscious.** Research in communication shows clearly that a large component of rapport is established non-verbally. To communicate more effectively we must be able to address the non-verbal element first. Not all of our communication lies within conscious awareness and the same is true for the person with whom we are communicating. Communicating respect and positive regard toward the other person non-verbally is therefore an important element to establishing good rapport.

- **The meaning of the communication is the response that you get.** This principle is about responsibility in the communication dance. We are assuming that if we do not receive the response we desire or expect, it is up to us to change our communication. Common sense tells us that it is easier to change our own behavior, than change that of others (tempting as it may be).

- **There is no failure only feedback.** The average person receives strong messages from very early around the concept of right and wrong — it is bad to be wrong and it is good to be right. This mind-set creates distinct limitations to our ability to communicate and learn. In one sense immediate success is much more limiting than failure because exploration ends with the success. Failure forces us to continue exploring the area for more information.

In response to a question about becoming discouraged after 700 failed attempts to create the light bulb, Thomas Edison replied, "I have not failed once. I have succeeded in proving that those 700 ways will not work. When I have eliminated the ways that will not work, I will find the way that will work."

- **Behavior is the highest quality information.** Every moment of every day people are giving you huge amounts of information about their response to your communication. Most of this process goes on unconsciously. It is tempting to focus only on making sense of their words. The words comprise only a small portion of the total message; body language and voice tone make up a surprisingly large portion of the complete message.
- **If what you are doing isn't working, do something different.** This is directly linked to the assumption about failure and feedback and the meaning of your communication. If you are not getting your point across, it is time to change what you are doing so that you can get a different result. More of the same (repeating or speaking louder) very rarely achieves the desired result.

Instead of assuming the other person "just doesn't get it" — take a different approach.

These assumptions can have a real effect on how we communicate. For a start, if we do not get the result we want, we are more capable of taking a different approach; instead of assuming the other person "just doesn't get it". This brings us back to our own flexibility (which we explore in chapter 7). In other words, assuming that there is something we can do about the way we are communicating is much more useful than trying to get the other person to change their way of understanding.

Teeter-Totter Topic

All communication is a balance between *relationship* and *information*. In business, as in any other area, effectively communicating with another person requires there to be enough relationship to balance the importance of the information. Professional speakers have an old saying that goes "no one cares how much you know, until they know how much you care". This principle is equally valid for general professional conversations. If there is insufficient relationship, the other person(s) will not care enough about the information you are trying to convey. On the other hand if there is only relationship and no information, no real progress can be expected from the conversation. Everyone has experienced meetings where the relationships were great and yet very little was achieved. All of the energy went into building and enjoying the relationship; little or nothing into the information aspect.

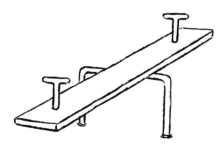

Generally the more important the information, the more imperative it is that the relationship aspect is cared for. When we are under pressure we frequently forget or accidentally drop the relationship piece. Our own emotional state is important; managing it when the stakes are high can help direct the conversation in a resourceful direction. When we are anxious about how a message will be received, we can tip over into information-only mode. If we are in a nervous and agitated state, we will communicate this to the other person non-verbally. Indeed, they may be so impacted by that non-verbal message that they don't notice the verbal message. So we must remember that non-verbals become strong messages in their own right.

When we take ownership of the teeter-totter and ensure we hold the balance between information and relationship, we rapidly become a more effective communicator. Look closely at very effective communicators and notice how they manage this balance carefully.

Connecting in a Different Way

The balance between information and relationship becomes even more important when the information has the potential for damaging the relationship between the people communicating. A study was conducted with senior executives as they prepared to retire from their positions. One of the questions the study asked them was to identify the most stressful part of their jobs. One might expect the executives to talk about big deals or crucial mergers. This was not the case. Invariably, the group surveyed talked about the stress of having to let people go, and of delivering bad news. I think what this says about communication in business life is that it is not always true when people say, "it's nothing personal it's just business" (true Godfather-style). It is a natural human tendency to not wish to disappoint others. The question is what can we do when we have disappointed others?

Flemons, in his book *Completing Distinctions*, talks about how couples deal with an affair that occurs during their relationship. He states that, "an affair cannot be forcefully forgotten, cannot be banished from the history of a relationship, but it can be *connected to* in a different way." In other words, they have discovered another way to communicate with it, which in turn enables them to communicate differently with each other.

Similarly, people within organizations cannot change how they are relating to each other if they are unwilling to connect to others in a different way. Holding grudges is often a psychological strategy people use to defend themselves from future hurt. However the strategy can backfire. A story from southeast Asia relates how the jungle dwellers used to catch monkeys.

The story goes that they would put a fig into a narrow-necked earthen jar and leave it at the base of a tree the monkeys frequented. The curious monkey would put its hand into the jar and grab the fig. As long as it held onto the fig, it couldn't get its hand out of the heavy jar. The monkey's ability to escape was hampered by the thing it was holding onto and easily caught by the jungle people. The moral of the story is that it's unwillingness to let go cost the monkey its freedom. We need to ask ourselves what are we holding onto that is preventing us from moving on. Holding on can happen in teams when members are unable to let go of things that have happened in the team's history. As a result they are hampered by their history.

Is Orion Always There?

When I think of changing interpretations of an event, constellations come to my mind. Consider the constellation of Orion in the northern hemisphere — the magnificent hunter of the winter night sky.

> *We are pattern recognition systems — we impose patterns and, by doing so, we also impose meaning.*

The configuration of the stars has represented Orion the Hunter for thousands of years. Yet if we traveled a few light years toward it we would find that the hunter has disappeared. The stars have not moved — we have and everything is different. Before we made the journey those eight stars depicted Orion and yet further out in space they mean something different. We are walking pattern recognition systems — we impose patterns and, by doing so, we also impose meaning. We are the meaning makers and how we make those meanings, shapes the way we communicate.

A more useful question to consider about an event or experience could be "How can I relate to this in the most resourceful and useful way?" or "What is the most useful meaning I can choose from what they said?" This implies there are a number of ways the event can be interpreted and that we have choice, rather than "what does that mean?" which implies there is one meaning that we have to discover.

Types of Communication

All communication can be effectively divided in to two types:

- *Intra*personal — the way we communicate with ourselves and
- *Inter*personal — the way we communicate with others.

Without adequate awareness and skill at the *intra*personal level, it is impossible for someone to be effective at the *inter*personal level. A house without a foundation may appear sturdy, however, when storms rage, it becomes a liability and dangerous to everyone inside it.

Intrapersonal Communication

According to the National Science Foundation the average person generates approximately 12,000 thoughts per day. It is reasonable to assume that most of us "talk" to ourselves at least as much as we talk to anyone else; this emphasizes the importance of the quality of our intrapersonal communication (self talk). Unfortunately, the majority of self talk is unconscious and is therefore operating below the radar.

GO DEEPER
Self Talk: www.anthillsite.com

High levels of motivation and clarity rely heavily on the kind of message being communicated internally. Negative messages or jumbled contradictory self talk lead to demotivation and lack of affirmative action. Becoming aware of the nature of self talk is the first step to changing it.

The simplest awareness device on the market is an elastic band. Placed on the wrist, it reminds us that thoughts matter. Twanging it when negative thoughts surface helps to begin the process of rewriting the scripts we run in our minds.

Our personal resilience is a reflection of the thoughts we have about ourselves and the world in which we live. If we wish to strengthen our own internal resilience, we must first check what thoughts we are running. Of the 12,000-odd thoughts we have each day, very few are critically examined. Most go unchecked or explored for relevance. We know in our heart of hearts that change is a constant and that the world in which we live today is not the world we lived in last year. Yet so many of the assumptions formed a year ago are still running our thoughts. They are fundamental to the quality of our lives.

Interpersonal Communication

As we work on further improving the quality of our internal communication, we can also work on the nature of our *inter*personal communication (communicating with others). One of the most important areas where we can improve our capacity to successfully communicate with others is with our voice tone. Voice tone plays a significant part in expressing meaning. Remember when you were young — the tone of voice your mother or father used could have a devastating effect. Unconsciously we use voice tone as an important part of the context of verbal information.

A great deal of our communication today is conducted over a phone and body language has little impact on how our messages are interpreted. On the phone the tone of our voice becomes the most important source of extra information (meta messages) about what is being said. Our voice tone is affected by our emotional state and this explains why emotional self-mastery (chapter 3) is so important. We may think we can mask or hide strong emotions such as anger or excitement from the other person, but the truth is we are communicating our emotions unconsciously all the time. Assuming this to be true, it becomes important to decide what emotional state we want to be in when communicating with a particular person or in a specific situation. The skills explored in chapter 3 will enable you to achieve greater emotional self-mastery. The saying that "to master others first master yourself" could be altered slightly to say "to master your communication, first master yourself".

Communication at the Speed of Light

Light travels very fast — 186 thousand miles per second, to be precise. Sound travels at a fraction of this speed — 750 miles per hour. We have all witnessed thunderstorms and know that we see lightning long before the sound of thunder reaches us. So when you say something, information about what you look like as you say it arrives much sooner than the actual words.

When "light and sound" messages match in content we call this *congruence*. Congruent messages are much more effective than messages that don't match or that are at odds with each other. It is important for us to be congruent in our communication by ensuring our non-verbal messages match our verbal ones. Saying we are pleased to see someone when we have a doubtful look on our face is an example of incongruence. Highly influential communicators also ensure their voice tone closely matches the verbal message they are sharing.

When someone responds poorly to something we said, we frequently think it was the words we used. Rarely do we think that it had anything to do with the other messages added to the words — the way we look or the tone of our voice.

The expression "you cannot *not* communicate" represents an interesting assumption in relation to emotions and voice tone. When we are annoyed with someone and we allow that annoyance to affect our emotional state, in turn affecting our voice tone, the other person inevitably picks up on this information. This may then change the direction of the conversation when the person responds to the non-verbal messages (voice tone, body language), rather than the words themselves.

Good self-mastery enables us to control our emotions so that we are not adding unwanted emotional content to our communication. Tone of voice does not go entirely unnoticed at the conscious level — people will say, for example, "please don't use that tone of voice with me". At times like these it is important to separate what the other person said, from how they said it. One way to separate the two messages — the verbal and non-verbal — is to say, "The tone of voice you used makes me feel 'X'. Is that what you intended?" Often the other person is unaware that two messages were delivered. The question enables them to clarify what they meant. The process of building and maintaining rapport can now continue.

A great deal of communication challenges could be avoided if we practice checking or testing the meaning of the other person's message. One of the most powerful skills is *backtracking*, where we repeat back to the person what they said to check our understanding.

Does it Matter Who Is Responsible?

It is a natural human tendency to hold other people responsible for misinterpreting our communication. This can set off a chain of events (invisible at first) that could blow up into a misunderstanding, argument or worse. Some people find the assumption that "the meaning of your communication is the response that you get" very challenging. They may respond by saying, "that is so ridiculous. How can I be held responsible for how someone interprets what I say?" Actually the point of the assumption is not where the responsibility lies, but where the opportunity for adjustment lies. We cannot really do anything about someone's ability to comprehend what we are saying. What we *can* do, is adjust how *we* are saying it. Highly effective communicators take responsibility for the effect their communications have and adjust how they say things when they find themselves misunderstood.

Team rapport is achieved when everyone is playing the same tune. Achieving and maintaining group rapport can be a challenge as rapport tends to ebb and flow. The secret is being able to maintain enough rapport for the team to function fully, at all times. Team rapport should not be mistaken for some kind of "group think". Rather it is based upon a willingness to embrace diversity of thought and a healthy amount of disagreement. General Patton is famous for the expression, "If everyone is thinking alike, then someone isn't thinking." Differences are valuable; it is how they are assimilated by the team that is important. Diversity brings with it multiple ways of responding and strong problem solving capabilities which is the main facet of all resilient systems.

A team in rapport is much more resilient and productive than one that is not. Team-building exercises are a great way to build team rapport. However, after the training session or team retreat is over, resilience is maintained day-to-day through good communication skills. All human behavior can be modeled. In other words if you can, I can and if I can, you can. This applies to communication skills. They can be developed further with specific skill-building exercises included at the end of this chapter.

> *Differences are valuable; it is how they are assimilated by the team that is important.*

Most of the time rapport is established unconsciously. We can also do certain things to accelerate the process or deepen its effect. Typically rapport is achieved by the exchange of a number of non-verbal messages. The exchange occurs within the first few seconds of meeting. The initial impression that is formed by people is based almost completely upon these messages. Some people are very effective at creating great first impressions. This is not an accident, although they may have no idea how they do it. On close examination, they send a specific set of non-verbal messages (a smile or a specific tone of voice for example) that helps establish rapport quickly.

People Like Us

The first step in building rapport is matching the other person. People like people like themselves and the more you make yourself like the other person (though tattoos last a long time) the easier it is for them to like you. With that attraction comes some very valuable attention that will ensure they listen to what you are saying. Body language is the most visible way you can match another person. Body posture, movements, and rhythm all fit in here. You don't have to be Robin Williams to match another person with your body. You *do* have to get over the idea of it — and using the words "mimic" or "imitate" does not help you here at all. The whole purpose of matching the other person is to honor or to meet them where they are and only to a level that you can feel comfortable also.

When you watch people closely in public places, such as malls and cafés, you begin to recognize the dance of rapport. Another way of thinking about this is that there is a natural tendency toward entrainment between people. Given the chance we automatically get into "synch" with each other. It happens unconsciously and most frequently between people who like each other already.

The matching I refer to here also applies to voice speed, tone and volume. Of these, speed is probably the easiest to match. People generally talk at the speed at which they think. So what does this suggest? If we wish to help the other person comprehend what we are saying, it makes sense to listen carefully to the speed they talk and match that speed. Too fast and they will not pick everything up, too slow and their mind will wander which can be just as harmful.

I See You

The South African greeting "*Sowabona*" means "*I see you*". When someone says "*Sowabona*" to you the customary reply is "*Ngikona*" or "*I am*". Because you see me, really see me, I am. In other words you are saying "you exist", "you have value". Sometimes we have been so long in a system (e.g., a family, church, or school) that it is almost as if we have become invisible. The system has habituated to our presence. At such times it is tempting to treat those around us as if they too were invisible. Few things could be so detrimental to our ability to effect change and live a productive personal or professional life. Matching another's body language is a strong subliminal message to the other person that you "see them".

Attention-Getting Behaviors

After establishing rapport, the next task is to gain and hold the other person's attention. You don't have to be talking all the time to hold their attention. Listening carefully enough so that you hear what they are saying is a great way to guarantee their attention. Good listening is about making your own mind quiet while they talk. If you have not tried this before, give it a go. Make your mind quiet (harder than it sounds — and practice pays off) while the other person speaks. The first thing that tends to happen is that we panic that we will not have anything intelligent to say when it is our turn. There is a natural tendency to want to impress the other person with what we have to say. Personal experience has taught me that one of the most reliable ways to impress the other person is to really hear what they say. You may be the first person who has really listened to them for a long time.

> *The wisest person in the room is the one who knows when to listen and how to listen.*

Really listening to another person in a group setting can be a challenge. There is so much going on and we may have our own agenda we wish to have addressed. However in such situations thoughtful listening is just as important as thoughtful talking. The wisest person in the room is the one who knows when to listen and how to listen.

The Benefit of Great Listening

A client once complained about having to take people from their work to have them trained in running effective meetings. What he did not dispute was that their meetings had been quite ineffective in dealing with ongoing departmental challenges. We did a rough estimate of how much money was being "invested" in their ongoing meetings. Calculating the total of the hourly rates of the 11 people attending the meeting (and without factoring in lost productivity because people were not at their desks) came to $4,500 per two-hour meeting. Held twice a month, this amounted to over $90,000 as an annual investment. At this point in the calculations we both realized that making their meetings more effective would be a very good investment.

We explored the dialogue process with this client. Before long everyone in the team began to talk about things that really mattered to them. They were also doing this in a way that was respectful of other people's opinions. This process has been championed by William Isaacs in his book *Dialogue and the Art of Thinking Together*. He and his partner, Juanita Brown, have also used dialogue (and permutations of the method) extensively with their corporate clients for all sorts of purposes. Their model of dialogue consists of four elements.

1. Listening
2. Respecting
3. Suspending
4. Voicing

1. Listening

This is a simple process that we all think we are so good at. Yet as we listen to another person it is so easy to add inferences to the things people say. When we do this, we also move into a judging mode that may affect what we hear and what we don't. In this way judgments can act as filters. When we allow this to happen we are not hearing the other person, we are only hearing our *inferences* about what they said.

2. Respecting

Respecting people's right to voice their opinion is easier in principle than in real practice. The more significant the disagreement between people (international disagreements, for example), the more important it is that the parties involved can respect each other's opinions. Isaacs describes the process of respecting as "making room for all the perspectives and voices without trying to get rid of any of it". If you practiced the perceptual positions exercise in chapter 2 you will have realized that perspective can have a tremendous effect on how people relate to their world.

3. Suspending

Suspending is the process of allowing a topic or theme to be suspended like a pendulum in the middle of the conversation. Suspending allows doubt to exist around the topic. It also prevents participants from falling into certainty and to access their ignorance more effectively. Exploring what we don't know is not always comfortable, according to Isaacs. Dialogue will be difficult for people "who know what they think and why they think it". Suspending also helps participants to broaden their attention to other aspects of the issue being discussed. In other words, we are expanding our awareness of other people and how they relate to the important issues.

4. Voicing

The fourth and final element of dialogue can be the most challenging. It requires us to speak our truth irrespective of who else is listening. Voicing also involves finding our own voice. It is so easy for us to speak from memory, saying the same old things we have said maybe a thousand times. To speak about something in the moment without knowing exactly what is going to come out, can be a challenge. Doing so can also provide a liberating model for others present. Finding our voice can also enable us to say something that is deeper and truer for everyone present. At this point we are tapping into the collective intelligence in the room, the things that the group wants to speak.

GO DEEPER
Dialogue: www.anthillsite.com

Commitment Versus Compliance

Leaders often refer to the challenge of achieving buy-in from their teams. Often this has been caused by the fact that people felt they had insufficient input. Within a top-down organization this can be a major challenge. A manager receives a mandate from above to achieve something. No one had played a part in forming this strategy and, therefore, had no sense of ownership as a result. Now the manager has the challenge of selling this idea to the people he leads. It is understandable that some managers apply the same strategy with those who report to them — drop the project on their lap.

An organization operating like this will have problems engaging its people in projects and initiatives. All is not lost, however. We can choose to engage our people through dialogue and through the engagement that comes from dialogue. Conversely, if they have had no opportunity to play a part in the creation, they are naturally going to be left wondering why they should support it.

> *People support what they create.*
> — MEG WHEATLEY

In the book *Presence*, Peter Senge states that "engineers know that the best technical solutions often fail to be implemented, or are not successful when they are, because of low trust and failed communication." So improved team communication goes beyond warm fuzzy feelings about team members. There are concrete business reasons why it pays to have people deeply involved in creating solutions to team challenges. According to Isaacs, dialogue achieves high levels of collaboration (collaborative intelligence) "by deepening the glue that links people together. This 'glue' is the genuine shared meaning and common understanding already present in a group of people. From shared meaning, shared action arises." This is effective communication in action. At the end of the chapter you will find an outline of the dialogue process that can be used to great effect in a multitude of business environments.

In an amazingly compact book, *The Thin Book of Naming Elephants*, Sue Annis Hammond and Andrea B. Mayfield claim that within a team setting there are three things that are required for team communication to be effective. They are (p. 92):

"1. being curious about how every other person sees the world;

2. respecting each person's perspective of the world as unique and essential to the group's success; and

3. making sure every person has a chance to speak and be heard."

These factors rely on each other. Some teams practice some of them and expect great cooperation from everyone. Unfortunately without all three only partial communication (and consequently cooperation) is possible.

Teams that "Speak Their Truth"

I used the dialogue process with a team of managers within a Canadian health care system recently. One person said, "I love this — I feel I have the chance to say things I have never felt permission to say before." After that expression, others in the group took the permission and said what they also felt. The end result of the session was a group that reached a place they had not been before in terms of closeness and commitment. They had taken the opportunity to share their assumptions and feelings about the team and about the problems they faced. Sharing assumptions is something we have already visited in chapter 1, but doing so within the team setting can improve communication considerably.

Meg Wheatley, in *A Simpler Way*, refers to a group of managers who shifted their definition of "information as power" to "information as nourishment". This helped to remind them that information is essential to everyone, and that those who have more of it will be more intelligent workers than those who are starving. The process of dialogue helps that nourishment to reach everyone.

David Isaacs and his partner Juanita Brown also evolved the "conversation café" from the dialogue process. Conversation cafés are used to explore topics in a public setting. In their book *The World Café — Shaping Our Futures Through Conversations That Matter*, Brown and Isaacs share a simple version of the collaborative dialogue process. This can be used in any situation where a group of people wish to address challenging issues.

GO DEEPER
Conversation Café: www.anthillsite.com

That's a Good Question

One of the central themes of all these approaches to enhancing communication effectiveness is the quality of the questions generated. A good coach asks good questions and a great coach asks great questions. Peter Block has written a splendid book on asking good questions. In *The Answer to How is Yes*, Block contests "We define our dialogue and, in a sense, our future through the questions we choose to address. Asking the wrong question puts us in the philosopher's dilemma: We become the blind man looking in a dark room for a black cat that is not there."

On the other hand asking the right question can have a miraculous effect whether we are trying to help a friend or facilitating a team meeting. A sign that you have asked a good question is the other person saying, "That's a good question". They are usually silent for awhile after that because your question has caused them to think new things. Good questions focus our attention and at the same time invite a deeper exploration of the issue. The structure of the question determines the direction our attention goes. Because of this, it is important that the question is a positive one. Problem-focused questions will help us spend more time with the problem, but not necessarily bring us closer to a solution.

GO DEEPER

Good Questions: www.anthillsite.com

In the *Encyclopedia of Positive Questions*, the authors (Diana Whitney, David Cooperrider, Amanda Trosten-Bloom and Brian S. Kaplin) have provided an entire book devoted to positive questions that can be used in a variety of situations. To help people appreciate the benefits of positive questions they suggest asking the following question (abbreviated version) at the beginning of a team meeting: "Reflecting back on your entire career think about the most memorable team experience you have ever had…Tell me…about the time when you were part of a really great team? What made the team a success?"

After people have had the opportunity to discuss this question for ten minutes in pairs, they are asked to report back about the experience. One thing that commonly happens is the energy in the room rises noticeably. When asked to report back about the effect the question had, participants typically report how inspired and deeply connected they felt. The authors of the *Encyclopedia* use these kind of questions as one of the major interventions in their Appreciative Inquiry (AI) approach to organizational change.

WHERE WE'VE BEEN

In this chapter we have explored how relatively simple and easy adjustments to our communication style can help us to be more effective in influencing others. The main points of this chapter are:

- Influence and manipulation are two sides of the same coin; the only difference is the intent of the communicator and that is our responsibility.

- What we assume about communication and other people has a tremendous effect on how successful (or otherwise) our communication can be.
- All communication contains the dynamic of information-and-relationship; managing this dynamic is the secret to creating productive and positive results.
- There is often a huge difference between what people say and what they mean; getting below the surface is vital to successful communication.
- Some information travels at the speed of light, others at the speed of sound; the right non-verbal cues can enhance our communication effectiveness.
- Listening is an attention-getting behavior; great listeners are great communicators.
- Dialogue is a powerful communication process.
- Questions are the most powerful way to connect with others and build rapport; they are also our most potent ally in influencing others.

 ## WHERE WE'RE GOING

With great communication comes the opportunity to develop great connections with other people, teams, and departments. Connection is the theme of the next chapter. Some of the questions we address in chapter 5 are: How important is connection? How can we achieve deep connection within a team? What part does collaborative intelligence play in flattened organizations?

CQ Tool© 4

*Exploring the Conversation Café**

One of the ways highly effective communication can be achieved in a team is through deep dialogue. It is common for organizations and teams to discover that although they thought themselves to be good at communication, they were, in fact, only utilizing a small portion of their potential in this area. Conversation Cafés adapt two ancient traditions: the talking-stick circle and deep dialogue. The talking stick ensures that only one person talks at a time and deep dialogue provides the opportunity for participants to speak to their own truth in meaningful ways. Dialogue also creates an environment that enables those involved to think together about a topic.

Prior to running the conversation café process, it is important to have an orienting question that people speak to as a catalyst for the conversation. An example for a team involved in providing customer service might be "What would it take for us to be able to surprise and delight our customers?"

*Special thanks to those at conversation café for their kind permission to use this guideline for the conversation café process <www.conversationcafe.org>.

Note: At least 50 minutes should be allowed for the process. It helps to have someone to volunteer as facilitator to keep a gentle eye on the process. Also it is useful to have someone acting as a recorder for the conversation, keeping track of the themes that emerge. Both of these roles should not prevent the volunteers from participating fully in the conversation.

STEP 1: The facilitator begins the session by reading out the six Agreements — six principles common to most dialogue and conversation cafés.

- Suspend judgment as best you can.
- Respect one another.
- Seek to understand rather than persuade.
- Invite and honor diversity of opinion.
- Speak what has personal heart and meaning.
- Go for honesty and depth without going on and on.

STEP 2: A simple process: A "talking stick" (any object that has been designated for the task) is passed around the group in a clockwise or counter-clockwise fashion. Only the person holding the talking stick may talk. Once they have finished they hand it to the person next to them. Two rounds of speaking without interruption introduce a quality of listening and reflecting that opens people to themselves and one another. People can pass if they like. They can be silent as their way of speaking. Then a lively conversation happens, keeping in mind the agreements to inquire rather than assert and debate. At the end, a final "talking stick" round anchors for each participant the gems they are taking away.

STEP 3: At the end of the session participants are asked to reflect on the process they have just experienced and share their thoughts. They are also asked to comment upon anything that emerged in the conversation which surprised them.

5

Connection

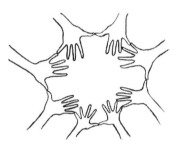

*Relationships are the essence
of the living world.*

GREGORY BATESON

Whether it is two cells sharing information or two nations negotiating international trade, connection is an essential factor in how things play out. Communication is impossible without connection and in many respects it is the core issue of this book. Connection makes communication possible; communication makes collaboration possible which further enhances the state of connection. Connection is a fundamental principle of all living systems and this includes all those that make up human society (teams, organizations, etc.).

In this chapter we explore how important connection is in building resilient teams and at the same time further enhancing our own Collaborative Intelligence (CQ). We will also look at the part CQ will play in the increasingly flattened structures of modern companies and the resilient teams that are required to make the whole thing work.

Daniel Goleman's work around the concept of Emotional Intelligence (EQ) was a major step forward in the thinking of how we operate as human beings. EQ is especially important because of the extent to which it was accepted by the business community. The concept of EQ has already made its way through early-adopters and into the mainstream. It is time for another set of skills to be introduced — based upon the ability to collaborate.

GO DEEPER

Emotional Intelligence: www.anthillsite.com

Celebrating Interdependence Day

Our universe is built on relationships. Relationships outnumber people and create the matrix (social, physical, and psychological) in which we live. Quantum mechanics shows us quite clearly that everything is connected to everything else. Physicists assure us that at the quantum level everything is energy and relationships. Connection is an important aspect of our world. Connections between nations, organizations, groups, team members, individuals, parts of individuals, even the chemicals that make up the human body are arranged in complex systems of interdependent relationships. The level of interdependence is deep and pervasive, yet people, teams, and organizations so often believe they can act with total independence.

Biologist Lynn Margulis comments that, "independence is a political concept, not a biological concept. Everywhere life displays itself as complex, tangled, messy webs of relationships." In natural systems disconnection and isolation usually represent dysfunction. The simplest definition of cancer is abnormal or uncontrolled cell division where some part of the body ignores the shared interests of the rest of the body. The isolation has become a manifestation and the cause of dysfunction.

Maybe some day we will evolve to the extent that there will be a holiday to celebrate interdependence rather than independence. The holiday could be a public acknowledgment (and celebration) of how interdependent we really are.

> *Life did not take over the globe by combat,*
> *but by networking.*
> FRITJOF CAPRA

We live in a world that is not only changing but the rate of change is accelerating. A tsunami of change is creating a world that places tremendous pressure on our individual ability to adapt. Resilience was earlier defined as the ability to bounce back and recover in harsh or challenging conditions. Certainly, we are all going to have to become more resilient to handle what is ahead of us. A healthy level of connection is an important factor in developing resilience. This is just as true for teams as it is for the organizations they serve. This makes CQ a vital area of concern for individuals and teams that wish to develop deeper, more reliable levels of connection within their organizations.

GO DEEPER
Resilience: www.anthillsite.com

CQ, Community and Organizations

We cannot talk about developing CQ within teams and organizations and ignore the importance of building community. Building a sense of community automatically expands the CQ of a group or team. Developing meaningful participation develops community. Chapter 7 will explore the theme of meaningful participation in greater detail. With the development of community within teams and organizations the CQ grows proportionally.

There are important lessons we need to learn about the development of community at all levels of society. At the micro level one of the issues that has become apparent and pressing is the shortage of skilled people and the challenge of retaining staff. An increasing number of business leaders are recognizing that one of the most cost effective ways of addressing these challenges is through the development of community within the workplace. No matter what the motivation, this is still a reassuring trend. From a business management perspective, people are less inclined to leave a community than they are an organization. A community is also a healthier place to work — the sense of support is beneficial to everyone's mental health especially when things get challenging.

A healthy corporate community is much more resilient than one that lacks the community factor. So far, this could be viewed as a cynical use of community — to simply address a business challenge. However, once community does begin to develop within businesses and teams it tends to transform the way in which business is conducted. The more connected people become, the more they realize the degree to which we

> *The more connected we become, the more we realize we are all part of a system that supports us.*

are all part of systems that support each other. The skills explored in chapters 1 through 4 enable the further development of CQ and this, in turn, increases the community building capacity of each individual.

Kazimierz Gozdz, in his *book Community Building*, explores the connection between the creation of learning organizations and community building. According to Gozdz we can use a series of questions to ascertain the level of community active within an organization. Here are some he uses.

- Is the organization moving toward greater inclusivity of information, people, and ideas?
- Is the organization sharing power effectively, becoming more consensual and democratic?
- At the organizational level, is the community becoming more capable of contemplative learning?
- Is the organization a safe place, a practice field, for exploring each person's full potential?
- Can the group fight gracefully?
- Is the group moving toward or away from becoming a group of all leaders?
- Is there a spirit of interconnectedness present?

What would the answers be to these questions for your team, department, and organization? Assuming that not all of your answers are what you would like them to be, how can we change this? Technology provides some of the answers.

George Por, Founder and Chairman, CommunityIntelligence Ltd., states that technology can and should support the four functions that our biological systems provide. These are the following:

- communication;
- coordination;
- memory/knowledge management; and
- learning.

By helping us to develop these functions beyond our own biological capacities, technology is helping us to develop the CQ of organizations. This will enable us to manage the *social and knowledge capital* more effectively — assets so rarely considered in the business world. In other words, technology will play an important part in developing the CQ of groups and organizations.

In relation to the connection between technology, community, and resilience, Por states, "Resilience after all is determined by the ability of the group to sense what is going on in the environment (business and otherwise) and to be able to share ideas with itself about how best to respond to the information that is coming in." Collaboration software must service the four enabling functions in order that complex business groups can further develop and support "community". Literally thousands of highly effective virtual communities exist on the Internet already — a quick visit to Google will attest to that.

GO DEEPER
Social Software: www.anthillsite.com

Collaborating and Resiling

Al Siebert in *The Resilience Advantage* makes a wonderful observation about resilience. He says that rather than thinking of resilience as something someone has (like a smile or a cough), we should think of it as something someone does. For this he coined the term "resile" — a verb to describe when a person, or any system for that matter, expresses its ability to respond in a resilient fashion. Resiling is a verb or a "doing" word while resilience indicates something we have — a characteristic or quality. So it is with CQ, a group or team actively collaborates.

Watching CQ in Action

Think of a flock of starlings. In your mind's eye watch them swirl in the sky, thousands of individual birds creating an aerial dance that demands the coordination of millions of wing beats. On the surface their synchronization appears to be created by each bird's ability to respond to the movements of its neighbors. However, high speed film demonstrates a fascinating fact. These birds do not actually have the ability to physically respond to the flock. Their nervous systems are physically unable to respond in the timeframes that make the dance of the flock possible. This phenomenon is observed in a wide range of groups, schools of fish, swarms of insects, and even large herds of animals.

At a distance watching this group behavior, it would appear that there is some sort of mass mind in effect. In fact this is actually what some research scientists contend is at work. Biologist Rupert Sheldrake has put forward the theory of morphogenic fields to explain the mass mind or swarm intelligence that the creatures appear to be accessing. Sheldrake goes on to claim that by tapping into the morphogenic field the birds know which way the flock is going to turn. Morphogenic fields are created, according to Sheldrake, as a field of collective intelligence surrounding groups of living creatures.

Sheldrake is not alone in his search to make sense of this field effect. Other field theorists include Ervin Laszlo who puts forward the concept of an "Akashic Field". This is a much more comprehensive theory, attempting to explain the basic structure of the universe. The fundamental idea is roughly the same, however — a field of information into which all living creatures can tap, given the correct circumstances.

A slightly different example, and no less amazing, is the way certain insects build their homes. The termite, for example, builds the largest structures on earth (compared to the size of the builders).

They create intricate architectural wonders (complete with built-in air conditioning) as a group and yet there are no "termite architects" nor "termite engineers". The knowledge of how to construct these intricate structures resides within the entire population. Only as a group do they have this capability; it does not exist in the individuals. This is an example of emergence — the appearance of group behaviors that were not evident within the individuals making up that group.

Ants are another great example of individual creatures that manage to build and maintain complex colonies without the aid of any specialists or even formal leaders. In most species of ant, when there is something that needs to be done to serve the anthill, available ants switch tasks and simply get on with it. The abilities they have together do not exist in individual ants, another example of emergent properties. It could also be perceived as evidence that the group is forming some sort of morphogenic field into which each individual can then tap for guidance in relation to building the nest.

Remarkable examples of this kind of behavior are cited in *A Simpler Way* (Margaret J Wheatley and Myron Kellner-Rogers) and in *Emergence* (Steven Johnson). These books also represent fascinating explorations of how the group behaviors of insects provide useful insights and implications for human group behavior.

CQ and Fields

The reason we have ventured into field theories is that CQ could be considered to be a field of information that exists within groups. Developing CQ could be an important step forward for human beings and have significant implications for how we operate in groups, teams, and organizations. Individually ants are pretty stupid creatures, but collectively they are very smart. Human beings on the other hand are individually very smart and collectively, well? The question running through this entire book is, "What will life be like when we are able to emulate the ant by tapping into the fields of intelligence that already surrounds us?" As CQ rises so does our ability to access collective intelligence or tap into the fields Sheldrake and Laszlo are talking about.

Developing CQ is an important step forward for human beings.

When we are able to tap deeply into our CQ, the question will no longer be, "What can we do?" when faced with global and personal challenges. Instead the question will be, "What *can't* we do?" Developing our ability to merge our intelligences and then tap into that massive resource for the benefit of the group as a whole could literally transform how we live our lives and operate within teams and organizations.

Systemically Speaking

The systems approach is one of the five disciplines that Peter Senge champions for sustainable organizational change. "Systems thinking", as he puts it in his book, had been around for some time before Senge so aptly identified it as a way for business and society to create and respond to change. Based upon systems philosophy it promotes an understanding of the whole by examining the link and interactions between the elements that comprise the whole system. Systems thinking has given us a way of looking at how relationships are the building blocks of everything, including any group of people, whether it is a family or a multinational corporation. This approach enables us to predict more reliably the possible implications of making changes to parts of the system.

More specifically systems thinking permits us to better understand emergent properties. For example think of your car. All the thousands of pieces have their own properties and capabilities. None of them on their own are able take you down the highway. Yet when they are assembled together the emergent property is the ability to take you where you want to go. Another example is a whirlpool. It would be impossible to predict the emergence of this formation from the chemical or physical properties of water. The emergent property of a whirlpool comes into evidence when a very large number of water molecules come together in a specific arrangement. But what does an emergent property look like within human systems?

When a group of people are brought together to work as a team emergent properties appear. Individually the members have certain capabilities and characteristics. However, as every team leader knows, once you have several people working upon a single task a number of things happen. One of the most noticeable phenomenon is how important group dynamics become. How all these people relate to each other effects how productive they are. As far as emergent properties are concerned the team working together is able to solve problems that none of the individual members could.

Closer to home, and to the theme of this book, emergent properties become important when we consider developing CQ within teams and organizations. High performance can be considered an emergent property of a group of people working together in a certain way. For most organizations the $64,000 question is, "What are the conditions in which a team becomes high-performing?" One of the secret ingredients is to enable the individuals making up the team to tap into the field that is created by the team. As they do this the CQ of the group automatically increases. A refinement of the question could then be, "What can we do to enable teams to more effectively trigger the CQ of which they are capable?"

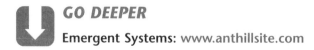

GO DEEPER
Emergent Systems: www.anthillsite.com

The Power of the Collective Relationship

The process of tapping into the collective mind has already been approached by a number of writers and researchers. In his book *Presence*, Otto Scharmer refers to a new type of collective relationship — one in which the individual is further enhanced rather than diminished. In Scharmer's words, the individual actually "connects …to one's highest future potential." A concern of many people when they first encounter ideas about collective intelligence or the collective mind is that they have to sacrifice their individuality and freedom of choice. Scharmer and the colleagues with whom he wrote *Presence* have tested this concept with a wide variety of groups and organizations. Their evidence points to the emergence of a collective mind (Sharmer's term for CQ) in which individuality is strengthened and enhanced rather than suppressed.

The synchronicity of firefighting, police, and emergency response teams cited earlier are good examples. Individual members of such teams refer to how they felt part of a single mind focused upon a single objective; invariably the experience is remembered as an extremely self-enriching and positive one.

Village Idiot and Collective Genius

Howard Bloom gives us a wonderful example of the power of CQ among our closest relatives in nature. In his book, *Global Brain*, Bloom compares the behaviors of chimpanzees and baboons. Chimpanzees are more intelligent than baboons; they even make their own tools. This latter fact further highlights the development of their individual intelligence. Comparatively the baboon is the village idiot when left to operate in isolation from the pack.

On the other hand, collectively baboons have achieved status as "the most widely distributed non-human primate" in Africa. In fact

they have been described as the "rats of Africa", flourishing in an environment where their smarter chimp-cousins are rapidly disappearing. So what are the factors contributing to the baboon's success?

One of the most striking differences between chimps and baboons is that although the chimps have more advanced brain capacity, baboons have much better developed social networks. While chimps live in groups of approximately 40, baboons congregate in troops of three to six times that size. One of the additional advantages of larger groups is that the pack provides greater protection from attack to individual members. In larger groups there is also a much more expansive social database of knowledge and, I would suggest, greater CQ at work. Collaboratively baboons are geniuses when compared to the individually smarter chimp. Because of their larger network they can gather greater quantities of information about their environment and adapt to changes more rapidly. Their capacity to summon the CQ within their troop has then very distinct (and life saving) advantages.

> *Collaboratively baboons are geniuses when compared to the individually smarter chimp.*

What baboons are achieving shouldn't really be a surprise. Our own ancestors discovered the strength-in-numbers principle very early. Picture the moment in time when our cave-dwelling ancestors figured out that taking down a hairy mammoth was going to require a large group of fairly well coordinated individuals. Even the African expression "it takes a whole village to raise a child" reminds us that people have relied upon networks to care for the precious things in life. In our modern society the importance of connection is being forgotten or lost in many places. When that occurs there is a disconnection from the collaborative intelligence that has served us so well throughout the evolution of our species.

In *Bowling Alone*, Robert Putnam catalogs a steep drop in the levels of participation with others, as displayed by Americans. The examples of civic disengagement are disturbing — neglected children, faltering education, spreading mistrust, ill health, income and wealth inequality, religious insularity, and disrespect for the law. This change also displays a shift in our collective values. A shift that may actually be the source of a great many of our social problems. With disconnection comes dysfunction it seems. This is just as true of organizations and the teams within them.

On the bright side, more and more organizations are recognizing the advantages of developing community. Whether it is within municipalities and cities, or corporate endeavors, there is a growing awareness that if we are to solve problems collectively created, the solutions will be created collectively too. Additionally, the severe challenges our species face right now, are forcing people to think about systemic solutions rather than resorting to silver bullet responses.

GO DEEPER

Community Building: www.anthillsite.com

Top Down — Bottoms Up

Top-down hierarchical corporate structures are proving to be inadequate in the rapidly shifting business and world conditions. And the challenge of change is only increasing. Looking back, that highly effective troop of baboons could be considered as a single, adaptive learning system. Our definition of "adaptive learning system" is any entity that learns from its environment and adapts appropriately to the challenges presented. Christopher Meyer and Stan Davis, in *It's Alive,* have made an extensive study of the adaptive learning process and isolated the important elements. Applying these to the business world, they claim organizations must develop the following six basic features.

1. **Self-Organize.** Rather than top-down management, bottom-up processing should be allowed to govern how the business responds to its environment. This means that general principles should be allowed to affect how individuals solve problems instead of mandating specific responses.

2. **Recombine.** This refers to the cross-fertilization of ideas and solutions. The team should take full advantage of the diversity within the organization and recombine ideas and responses from throughout the entire system.

3. **Sense and Respond.** Enable the system to recognize significant changes and respond appropriately without having to refer to many layers of higher authority. According to this principle all parts of the organization act as a sense organ for change and responses do not have to be centrally coordinated.

4. **Learn and Adapt.** Continually learning from the environment and amassing a social database of successful adaptations will enhance the team. Adaptation is considered to be a continual process.

5. **Seed, Select, and Amplify.** Many options are tested and winning responses and adaptations are reinforced and amplified.

6. **Destabilize.** Elements of the random must be continually introduced to enable the system to be sustained in an alive and

adaptive state. Within this principle challenge is considered a welcome opportunity for re-invention.

Bottom-Up Businesses

An important distinction we must become aware of here is the difference between top-down and bottom-up processing. Top-down processing represents hierarchy and command and controls the information flow. Bottom-up processing, on the other hand, represents information flowing up from the grass roots of an organization. All of these features can be detected in a typical ant colony. This may explain why anthills are some of the most resilient communities within the natural world. Entomologists describe ant colonies as a system that lacks visible hierarchies of command, in other words they function in a bottom-up fashion. (See Figure 5.1 for a geometric explanation of the two processes.)

Figure 5.1
Bottom Up/Top Down

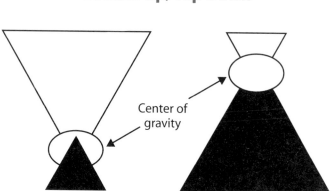

The question that should be asked is how can we use bottom-up processing more effectively within human organizations? There are lots of examples of the systematic use of this type of processing, such as the rating system used by Ebay. In the Ebay system members contribute to each others' reputation by rating the kind of interaction they had while conducting trade. The telephone/text message voting system established for television shows such as *American Idol* is another, granted less sophisticated, example of bottom-up processing. The point is that as the speed of change continues to accelerate, we must be able to learn and adapt more quickly. Bottom-up processing is one of the most prevalent ways natural systems respond to the challenge of change. The result of increasing the level of bottom-up processing will enable companies to achieve their business objectives with fewer levels of authority. Each individual is guided by a few basic principles that enable them to serve the greater good, in the best way possible at that particular point in time.

Meyer and Davis, in their book *It's Alive*, referred to leadership models used by Marines. In the book, they quote Colonel Van Riper, "We are very good at instilling certain behaviors in our Marines," Van Riper states. "They understand our intent, and intent is like an algorithm in a computer or DNA in a biological system…Now we must instill more tactical principles, so that instead of detailed prescriptive orders, everyone on the battlefield would inherently understand what to do. Building from the bottom up, we could have a much more powerful organization." Here is a great example of bottom-up processing within a human organization. Van Riper goes on to describe his leadership style as one that is "in command and out of control". This highly respected commander was essentially achieving his objectives by using the bottom-up intelligence of his troops. For most organizations a combination of top-down (via guiding principles) and bottom-up processes, enhanced by CQ, will be the best compromise (see Figure 5.1). The balance will depend on the organization and the circumstances. The two forces can be adjusted to provide the optimal mixture of direction or guidance and the ability to respond to environmental changes.

GO DEEPER

Bottom-up and Top-down Processes: www.anthillsite.com

Wise Teams

So what are the signs we could indentify that would tell us there was sufficient CQ within our team? In their book, *The Wisdom of Teams*, Katzenbach and Smith analyzed the reasons behind troubled teams and found they had certain common features. I have included some of my own conclusions after each point.

- **A weak sense of direction:** a sign that the top-down/ bottom-up dynamic was not very well balanced.
- **Insufficient or unequal commitment to team performance:** evidence that the CQ of the team was not high enough to create effective collaboration.
- **Critical skill gaps:** this probably boils down to insufficient or ineffective training.
- **External confusion, hostility, or indifference:** potentially a symptom of insufficient CQ within the organization. It could also be caused by poorly formulated or communicated (or both) team/organizational objectives.

There appears to be a trend pointing toward a lack of CQ. On the flip side of the coin, within high performing teams, Katzenbach and Smith discovered an emphasis on shared leadership roles. In contrast to clearly focused leadership roles, individual and mutual accountability was observed as much more important. This is a clear indication that CQ is an increasingly important factor in team performance.

If we raised our expectations then it wouldn't
take a crisis for us to experience the satisfaction
of working together.
MEG WHEATLEY

We Don't Need Another Hero

More and more organizations are realizing that what is not required is more heroes to save the day as far as their business performance is concerned. A hero concentrates the capacity for action around themselves and also tends to disempower everyone else (after all why would they have to do anything if someone was going to save them).

The DNA that Van Riper referred to negates the need for individual heroes. Rather everyone inherently knows what to do and that it is up to *everyone* to save the day. In *Guts*, the Freiburgs refer to a similar kind of guiding principle as the "heroic cause". They provide examples of heroic causes that have acted as the DNA, guiding the overall direction of employees' attention. Here are some from their book (p. 211).

- Southwest Airlines: We are in the business of freedom.
- Apple Computer: We want to educate the world.
- Fannie Mae: We help people achieve the American dream.
- Medtronic: We relieve pain, restore health, and give people longer lives.
- Schwab: We are the guardians of our customers' financial dreams.

Of course these statements are similar to vision statements but I'm sure you would agree that heroic cause has a much sexier ring to it. These grand callings elevate the significance of what people are achieving who work within the organization. We will visit this approach again in chapter 7 as a part of the exploration of meaningful participation — one of the most important emergent properties of teams with high CQ.

CoCreation Versus CoReaction

The choice of a heroic cause helps teams and organizations to *co-create* their reality by deciding what they want to have. The opposite of this is *co-reacting*, which is uncoordinated and ineffective group reaction to unfavorable or unwelcome elements of the environment. In true adaptive learning systems fashion, unexpected challenges should be opportunities for teams to discover more about themselves and the wide range of possible responses they have open to them. Teams with low CQ tend to see these as instances of inflexible and predictable patterns of problem solving behavior.

> *In true adaptive learning systems unexpected challenges are opportunities for teams to discover more about themselves.*

Remember if we always do what we have always done, we will always get what we have always got, and that might not be what we want.

The process of co-creation says that one of the best ways a group (especially business teams) can design their response to rapidly changing environments can be achieved by enhancing the quality of conversations. (This topic has been explored in chapter 4 — communication).

> *All change, even very large and powerful change, begins when a few people start talking with one another about something they care about.*
> MEG WHEATLY

Raising Arizona and Our CQ

Obliviously CQ is something we should be developing proactively in our places of work, rather than searching for when things have gotten out of hand. We have talked a lot about the importance of it in this book, and the question emerges again; "How do we raise the CQ of teams?" There are a number of approaches that can raise the CQ of teams. Three of the most robust approaches are the following:

1. Appreciative Inquiry;
2. Strength-Based Approach; and
3. Solution-Focused Thinking.

Looking at all three models we can see common threads in the principles behind each of them. They all take a positive approach toward people. They also all focus on creating something rather than getting rid of something. Let us look at each individually.

1. Appreciative Inquiry

As we've touched on before, AI was originated by David Cooperrider of Case Western Reserve University. It is rapidly becoming one of the most widely accepted models for evaluating and planning organizational change.

Appreciative Inquiry utilizes a four-stage process focusing on the points below:

1. **Discover:** The identification of organizational processes that work well;
2. **Dream:** The envisioning of processes that would work well in the future;
3. **Design:** Planning and prioritizing processes that would work well; and

4. **Deliver** (or *Create*): The implementation (execution) of the proposed design.

The simple act of looking for things to appreciate within systems is one of the key elements of this model. The appreciative filter is applied to all levels of the organization, right down to the individuals that make it up. Rather than being told there is something wrong with you or your team, the approach seeks out what you and your team are good at and focuses on building upon that. The AI approach relies heavily on the generation of questions that are designed to enable people to find things they are proud of and feel good about.

GO DEEPER

Appreciative Inquiry: www.anthillsite.com

2. Strength Upon Strengths

The second of the approaches we are going to examine is the *strength-based approach*. This has much in common with Appreciative Inquiry. As early as the 1950s the social work profession recognized the importance of identifying strengths in people. Building on people's strengths rather than focusing on their weaknesses achieves essentially the same thing as AI. The strength-based approach has been more recently championed by Marcus Buckingham in his book *Now Discover Your Strengths*. Buckingham's work in this area has been informed by the 17 years he spent with the Gallop Research Organization. According to Buckingham we achieve several things simultaneously when we build on people's strengths. We help the person build upon something they already have competence in, where their confidence is greatest. By focusing on these areas we are also building positive relationships within the organization which builds healthy levels of CQ.

3. Focusing on Solutions

The third approach is the *solution-focused approach.* This approach is about deciding what we want to have, rather than using our (finite) resources to try to get rid of what we do not want. The concept of creative tension that was referred to in chapter 3 is a central tenet of this approach. The first step in this process is deciding what we *do* want (rather than what we *don't* want) and focusing our energy upon that. According to Robert Fritz what we do want is the goal. This must be then compared with the present set of circumstances, referred to as the current reality. Some people mistake this approach for some sort of rose-tinted perspective toward problem solving. On the contrary if we do not acknowledge the brutal facts of the situation, we cannot establish creative tension. Without creative tension there will be no movement from what is to what is desired. As you can see there are strong similarities between all three approaches. The application of any or all of these will go a long way in raising the CQ within organizations and teams.

GO DEEPER
Solution Focused Thinking: www.anthillsite.com

Technology, Connection and CQ

Developments in technology have extended our ability to connect systems and create networks. The impact of the invention of the Internet has been comparable to that of the Gutenberg printing press. Both enabled a large number of people to affordably access vast amounts of information. What the Internet also provided was the ability to connect people with people rather than just people with information. The immense amount of fiber optic cable installed was a side-effect of the dot.com bubble and is one of the technological developments that have had significant social impacts. As a result of the physical networks set down, a huge matrix of virtual human networks have emerged. The bubble did indeed burst, however, and in its wake it left a huge physical network that has transformed the way we connect with each other and how we do business.

It seems increasingly obvious that technology, like IQ and EQ, is necessary but not sufficient for any organization to be able to adapt to the changes occurring in the business world. In the past many experts have claimed technology as a panacea for all our problems. This is not always the case. In conjunction with collaborative software, technology can help us further develop our CQ. Think about a spider's web for a few moments — a matrix of finely woven threads that are collectively (or collaboratively if you wish to view a spider's web as a metaphor) able to withstand tremendous pressures. Building teams that emulate this type of strength is what this book is about and technology has its part to play.

One of the most important ways humans express their CQ is through conversation — this has been true for literally thousands of years and has not changed substantially. With the Internet at their disposal millions of people are connecting (via chat rooms, forums or messenger services) with other people they have never physically met. With a population of one billion, the Internet has, in just ten years, become the "eighth continent". It represents the most pervasive form of technology in our society and is transforming the way we live our lives and how business is conducted. There should be no surprise then that it is considered to be a fundamental tool for developing the CQ of planet earth (as well as the businesses and teams that live here).

George Por in his article entitled "Quest" states that, "Organizations that will succeed in these times of accelerating changes will be social organisms with a collective intelligence to guide them through turbulence and transformations." CQ and technology will enable groups to tap into their Collective Intelligence more effectively. Por goes on to claim that in respect to social capital, "Maximizing the organization's human and intellectual capital is the key to success in the new, knowledge-based economy." In other words, the organization (or team) that can communicate and collaborate most effectively with itself and its environment will be the one that will thrive in these times of rapid change. In society and business "adapt and respond" will be the mantra for years to come. The impact that technology is having on CQ can be glimpsed by simply googling "collaboration + software" — over 100 million results appear. In the last few years there has been an explosion in the applications of technology in this area.

> *With a population of over one billion, the Internet has, in just ten years, become the "eighth continent".*

WHERE WE'VE BEEN

In this chapter we have explored the very heart of CQ — connection. The main points of this chapter are:

- Interdependence is a much more potent force than independence.
- CQ could be considered to be an emergent property of groups of people.
- Field theories may hold the clue to why none of us is as smart as all of us.
- Isolation tends to be dysfunctional while connection promotes healthy systems.

- Top-down and bottom-up processing are important forces and finding the optimal balance promotes high levels of CQ.
- There are positive alternatives to the old hierarchical methods for managing organizations.
- Technology is a strong ally in developing networks of connection and strengthening CQ.

WHERE WE'RE GOING

Building connection within teams, virtual and otherwise, may require assistance from technology; however everyone knows that it is only part of the story. Building connection through relationships is fundamentally about people discovering values that they share and the desire to do something to support those values. In the complex societies in which we operate, finding ways to honor our values and those of others often requires creativity. Finding ways to establish and develop collaboration also demands that we practice high levels of flexibility. Creativity and flexibility are the themes of chapter 6.

CQ Tool© [5]

Building Connection Through Appreciation

Appreciation is a powerful force within interpersonal relationships, teams and organizations. Any exercise that makes people more aware of its significance will have a positive effect. For example, when providing feedback to either an individual or a team that you are supervising, building appreciation into the feedback can achieve two specific things. First, it gives you an opportunity to attract attention to things that you appreciate about their performance. Second, you can connect this appreciation with a call for making specific changes to the performance.

One of the best ways to achieve this is by using the "feedback sandwich". The feedback sandwich places an appreciative statement about performance before and after a question related to improving or changing performance. Here is an example:

"John I really appreciated the way in which the summary of the report you submitted captured the spirit of our program. And I wonder what you could do next time to ensure the report is submitted on time? And also I noticed that you put a lot of care into the physical presentation of the report."

Notice in the statement that two appreciative statements sandwich a question focused on improvement. They are joined by the word "and" rather than "but". "But" tends to have a negative effect upon the listener as it distracts them from the

*element of appreciation and causes them to anticipate a neg-
ative or critical comment. The question in the middle clearly
indicates that an answer is required, and that responsibility
for action lies with the person receiving the feedback. By
answering the question they are more likely to take responsibility for making the changes necessary.*

STEP 1: In groups of three participants, take turns being
the person providing the feedback (A), the person receiving the
feedback (B) and the person observing the process (C).

STEP 2: The person providing some feedback, A, chooses a
context (e.g., someone is consistently late for work) and provides some feedback to that effect (e.g., "John you are always
late for work"). B notes what effect this has.

STEP 3: A now creates a sandwich of a question directed at
creating a change in their behavior, sandwiched by two appreciative statements, connected by the word "and". B notes the
effect this form of feedback has and compares the two. C ensures
A used the correct structure of the sandwich in the second
example and coaches A if adjustments are required.

STEP 4: The group rotates through the three roles until each
person has experienced each role.

STEP 5: As a group spend 5 to 10 minutes discussing the
advantages of the sandwich structure and places where it would
be particularly useful.

6

Creativity & Flexibility

Men are born soft and supple; dead, they are
stiff and hard. Plants are born tender and
pliant; dead, they are brittle and dry. Thus
whoever is stiff and inflexible is a disciple of
death. Whoever is soft and yielding is a disciple
of life. The hard and stiff will be broken.
The soft and supple will prevail.

LAO-TZU

Although on the surface our everyday world appears reasonably stable, extensive scientific research has uncovered a physical universe that is in continual flux, requiring constant adaptation. To have successfully emerged in such a universe, life has to be adaptive. The process of adapting and responding to change requires a generation of new creative solutions and this demands creativity. In this particular game, the price of failure is extinction.

Of the many myths that exist around creativity, one of the most prevalent must be that some people are creative and some are not. Truth be told, the very fact that we are living systems, ensures we are creative. The story of bacteria demonstrates clearly that creativity is a principle of nature rather than a recent discovery of Homo sapiens. Biologist Lynn Margulis describes changes that occurred on our planet approximately two billion years ago (Capra, *The Web of Life*, p. 241):

"In one of the greatest coups of all time, the (blue-green) bacteria invented a metabolic system that required the very substance that had been a deadly poison…The breathing of oxygen is an ingeniously efficient way of channeling and exploiting the reactivity of oxygen. It is essentially controlled combustion that breaks down organic molecules and yields carbon dioxide, water, and a great deal of energy in the bargain…The microcosm did more than adapt: it evolved an oxygen-using dynamo that changed life and its terrestrial dwelling place forever."

By being creative, life transformed a poison into an important ingredient for its own success. This highlights one of the most amazing facets of true creativity — the ability to turn a liability into an asset. This is also a wonderful example of collaborative intelligence — solving a problem by tapping into the combined processing capacity of the whole colony.

Turning liabilities into assets is a useful skill when it comes to dealing with human systems. An example of this could be a team handling large amounts of diversity (cultural, ethnic, etc.). In this instance the diversity could be considered a *liability* that must be overcome (e.g., developing a management style that works for everyone). When the diversity that exists within the team is turned into the capacity for the cross-fertilization of ideas, the problem-solving capacity of the team is expanded considerably. Diversity has been transformed from a liability to an asset.

CQ plays an integral part in this process of transforming liabilities into assets. If the members of that team were unable to collaborate deeply then possibly the liability would have remained.

Intelligent Bacteria

Eshel Ben-Jacob and James Shapiro, world-reknown scientists in the study of bacteria, have demonstrated that E. coli can learn how to switch from its preferred food source (lactose) to aspirin. This is a feat similar in kind that would be required for us to switch to the digestion of tinfoil. What enables this organism to display such amazing adaptability? Each of the trillions of E. coli in the colony are acting as individual problem solvers, with one very specific condition: they are all communicating intensely with each other. With trillions of separate information processors working (in parallel fashion) on the problem and immediately communicating the results they are getting, they *collaboratively* pull off the seemingly impossible. Although the IQ and EQ of an *individual* E. coli cell may be extremely low, the CQ of the *colony* enables it to do things that we humans would find very difficult, if not impossible.

CQ & Learning

I am curious what will be possible when humans have developed the CQ of our colony to the extent achieved by simple bacterium. Our level of creativity will have sky rocketed, as Ken Blanchard has pointed out, "None of us is as smart as all of us". How smart all of us can be is determined by our ability to collaborate at deeper levels than most of us do right now.

Peter Senge's concept of "learning organizations" touches upon this idea of collaborative intelligence although he does not use this term. Senge defines a learning organization as, "An organization that is continually expanding its capacity to create its future". Notice that survival is not mentioned. Learning (and the creativity that comes with it) is considered to be something that should be proactive and generative rather than reactive, based solely upon hindsight, or focused on surviving. There is also an obvious link between learning and creativity. Learning is not about having *access to information*. Learning is about what we *do with the information*. The scene has been set for the transition from the information age to the age of creativity.

> *Learning is not about having access to information.*
> *Learning is about what we do with the information.*

The Age of Creativity

John Kao, author of *Jamming*, states that we are already in the age of creativity because we are in the age of knowledge and creativity brings value to knowledge. According to Kao we are also in the age of creativity because the speed of change demands that we are able to reinvent ourselves (this is just as true for teams and organizations) and that requires creativity. Kao goes on to point out that the new role of management is that of emancipator of creativity, rather than controlling it.

Many companies have already recognized the tremendous value in creativity. This can be seen every time a large multinational buys up one of its smaller but more creative competitors. In this case the larger company is not so interested in the physical equity but rather the creative equity. It would make more business sense, in most cases, for organizations to encourage and nurture creativity within themselves, than buying it from outside.

Teams that exercise high levels of creativity are more resilient and learn faster and more effectively. So developing creative capacity within teams achieves many things at once.

No Two Alike

The natural world is so creative and so committed to the creative process that it doesn't like creating two of anything that are identical. Out of the six billion people living today, apart from identical twins, no two have the same DNA. So life loves to invent and reinvent. We are most in alignment with our own true nature when we are inventing and reinventing, particularly ourselves. Unless we are able to question some of the assumptions we make about ourselves, as we explored in chapter 1, we are unlikely to be able to do that. For instance, our assumptions also play a central role in how effectively we express our creativity. The assumption that you are not creative prevents you from accessing your creative self. This becomes a self-fulfilling prophesy with very significant implications. The same is true when we make *positive assumptions* about creativity. The creator of the Stanford Business School course on creativity, Michael Ray, shares three assumptions about creativity with every student.

1. Creativity "is essential for health, happiness, and success in all areas of life, including business."
2. "Creativity is within everyone."
3. Although it is in everyone "it is covered over by the voice of judgment."

> *To live a creative life, we must lose our fear of being wrong.*
> JOSEPH CHILTON PEARCE

Learning to be Uncreative

What we attend to expands and grows, so it is with creativity. Some of the limiting ideas that surround our creativity were formed during our formal education. I can't speak for each of you, but creative expression was not considered an important activity at the schools I attended. If we couldn't draw we were encouraged to focus our energy on other activities. The implicit message was "if you are not very good at something, don't do it". It did not occur to many people within the education system that a child might enjoy drawing whether they were very good at it or not. Doing something for its own sake wasn't considered to be time well spent. Simply put, for many people, if they were not naturally artistic, their creativity was not encouraged and they were pointed toward the sciences where rationality held office.

Individual creativity is important. Just as you cannot build a resilient team out of non-resilient individuals, you cannot make a creative team out of non-creative individuals. By more fully expressing their adaptability and flexibility — two of the most important aspects of creativity — team members are able to operate more creatively together.

> *The illiterate of the future are not those*
> *that cannot read or write. They are those that*
> *cannot learn, unlearn, relearn.*
> ALVIN TOFFLER

Creativity Versus Innovation

We should stop for a moment and make the distinction between creativity and innovation. Creativity is defined as the ability to create new ideas and things. Innovation is the application of creativity to practical problems. Another way to look at the difference is Michael Gerber's (*The E-Myth Revisited*) definition: "Creativity thinks up new things, innovation does new things." Business is obviously more interested in doing new things. The speed that change is occurring in society and business means the mantra for most industries is "innovate or evaporate". This probably explains why creativity is rapidly becoming a key factor in business success.

> The speed that change is occurring in society and business means the mantra for most industries is "innovate or evaporate".

Creativity and Flexibility

Creativity and flexibility are not only important elements of business competitiveness, they are also good for employee health and wellness and staff retention.

> *Flexibility and adaptability do not happen just by reacting fast to new information. They arise from mental and emotional balance, the lack of attachment to specific outcomes, and putting care for self and others as a prime operating principle. Flexible attitudes build flexible physiology. Flexible physiology means more resilience in times of challenge or strain. Staying open — emotionally — insures internal flexibility.*
> DOC CHILDRE AND BRUCE CRYER, *FROM CHAOS TO COHERENCE*

In chapter 5 we explored the significance of team alignment. However a team that is connecting deeply and aligning its energies will still fail to survive or thrive if it cannot exercise creativity and flexibility in the face of external challenges. In his book *Good to Great*, Jim Collins states, "The good-to-great companies faced just as much adversity as the comparison companies, but responded to that adversity differently." What was it that enabled them to respond differently? They were able to stop, take stock of what was happening, and *create* a response. The difference is the co-creation of a response to the challenge versus a knee-jerk co-reaction. Co-creation instead of co-reaction.

With all of the advantages that creativity brings, you would be tempted to think that the study of it as a tool within business has been going on for a long time. Not so. Only in the last 20 years has creativity become a formal part of the business school curriculum. So we have not been *consciously* applying the creative process within business for very long. This seems strange because healthy business is such an inherently creative process. All businesses have their origins with somebody and an idea they thought could be a business. The tricky part occurs when business people try to quantify the value that imagination (and creativity) bring to business. This may explain the uncomfortable relationship between the two. It's time to get over this and begin to embrace creativity and flexibility as important aspects of every business. One of the fundamental questions we must ask is, "How can we develop more creative and innovative teams?"

> *You never change things by fighting the existing reality. To change something, build a new model that makes the existing model obsolete.*
> R. BUCKMINSTER FULLER

Ways of Tapping into Creativity for Business

There are a number of factors associated with developing greater personal/team creativity and innovation and they are as follows:

- orientation toward the creative process;
- the role of great questions;
- specific techniques/processes; and
- use of humor.

Orientation

As mentioned before, the approach we take toward creativity and innovation, our own and that of others, has an impact on how successful we will be. From an individual perspective it may be worthwhile to take up a past-time that provides us an opportunity to express our creative side. It could be as simple as taking a water color class or learning to play a musical instrument. Learning a second or third language can also have very stimulating effects upon the human brain. Actions speak louder than words and doing something that requires we exercise our creativity can be a lot more effective than simply reciting an affirmation about it.

The Role of Great Questions

The way in which we define challenges can have a huge impact upon the way we relate to them. Therefore the questions we formulate play a pivotal role in framing the issue or challenge. More specifically great questions can do a number of things, including the following:

- determine whether we take a problem-focused or solution-focused approach;

- focus our attention on particular parts of an issue;
- stimulate new ways to think about something;
- direct the attention of others; and
- challenge hidden assumptions.

Each of these effects, in their own right, expands the creativity being employed. Formulating questions should be considered as a discipline and disciplines require practice. In this instance practicing the creation of great questions can pay significant dividends in terms of, for example, focused and productive conversations, more effective meetings, and greater clarity with executive decisions. Meg Wheatley has commented that we would all be better off with a "little more curiosity and a little less certainty". Certainty is very much like deep ruts in the snow, it will take us to very predictable destinations, often the ditch.

Some of the responsibility for our approach to asking questions lies with what we were taught in schools. Our educational system encouraged us to supply answers to predetermined questions, not to pose new questions. How much larger and more interesting would our conception of the world be if we had been taught to be experts at asking questions?

> *How much larger and more interesting would our conception of the world be if we had been taught to be experts at asking questions?*

Questions, then, link us to the very center of our creative selves. The bacteria mentioned at the beginning of this chapter was really addressing a question — a question related to its survival and discovering how to use oxygen rather then be poisoned by it was the bacteria's answer. Questions have been mentioned a great deal throughout this book because they play such a central role in enabling us to be more adaptable and resilient.

Because questions are intrinsically related to action, they spark and direct attention, perception, energy, and effort, and so are at the heart of the evolving forms that our lives assume... Questions function as open-handed invitations to creativity, calling forth that which doesn't yet exist.
MARILEE GOLDBERG

Questions play a role in understanding the assumptions at play in our lives and the teams in which we work (chapter 1). They help us explore how perceptions affect the way we respond to the world (chapter 2). The type of questions we are able to address will have an impact on our sense of self-mastery (chapter 3) and how effective our communication is with other people (chapter 4). We shall be visiting the theme of questions again in chapter 7, when we explore the topic of meaningful participation.

Use of Specific Techniques/Processes

There are literally thousands of processes and techniques for generating creative solutions to problems. Thousands of books have been written about creativity and how to expand it, personally or as a team, so we shall not explore that topic in depth here. One of the main ways to expand creativity is by exploring different perceptual perspectives. At the end of chapter 2 (perception) there was an exercise involving perceptual perspectives. These perspectives can also be used to explore a problem or anything about which you wish to be more creative. This process was developed by Robert Dilts and was originally modeled from the creativity strategies of Walt Disney. At the end of this chapter you will find the "Walt Disney Strategy" exercise and can explore its benefits in relation to expanding creativity.

GO DEEPER
Creativity: www.anthillsite.com

Role of Humor

There is an intimate relationship between "Aha" and "Ha-ha". Inherently all humor is based on some form of creativity. As people laugh, they breathe more deeply than normal and send greater quantities of oxygen to the brain. The human brain uses over 20% of the body's oxygen, so increasing the supply boosts performance significantly and helps learning. A great deal of humor relies upon changing perspectives (or frames of reference) and this is also an integral part of the creative process.

Humor plays a strong social function too. Almost all mythologies have a trickster or fool of some kind. One of the roles this character plays is to make fun of serious subjects, which provides a release of nervous tension. In this case the trickster is acting as a safety valve around important and potentially stressful situations. The trickster/clown appears often at the most important social/religious rituals. American Indian culture has the great rabbit, the coyote, the ravens, and the blue jay.

The fool appears in other cultures as a joker or jester. In such a position — masked and playing a part — they can provide valuable feedback to the ruling class because they are allowed to disregard the norms of the social order.

In the Sufi tradition, the wise idiot plays an important role in helping "seekers" to go beyond the logical mind. The story of Mulla Nasrudin and his lost coins in chapter 2 illustrates the point that we fail to recognize our own inherent creativity, simply because we are looking for it in the wrong place. The techniques and processes referred to earlier can help us begin to look in some of the right places for our own latent creativity.

Laughter is the jam on the toast of life. It adds flavor, keeps it from being too dry, and makes it easier to swallow.
DIANE JOHNSON

Creativity at Its Natural Best

It is becoming increasingly apparent that if teams and companies are to adapt to the rapid changes occurring in society, they will have to tap into their natural creative abilities and turn that capacity into innovation. Smart companies are already doing that.

Meyer and Davis provide a fascinating set of examples, in *It's Alive*, where companies have emulated the creativity and innovation of natural systems to build strongly adaptive businesses.

One example is the John Deere Company. One of their divisions manufactures seeders. The business challenge the company faced was that there were 1.6 million possible permutations for the configurations that could be ordered by customers. Trying to create a production schedule to optimize work hours and other resources was challenging, to say the least. John Deere used the services of a company called Optimax Systems. Using genetic algorithms Optimax would "breed" the various possible schedules to test for "fitness" — the fittest schedule would be the one the computers bred over night before each working day. Using powerful computers, the breeding process could be repeated over 40,000 times in a vastly accelerated version of natural selection. The results were so dramatic at John Deere that suppliers had trouble keeping up with John Deere's requirements and production schedules met target consistently.

So here we have an example of principles from natural systems (cross-fertilization) being applied to a real-life business challenge. Organic aspects of "adapt and respond" practices can be seen in the more recent developments of software design. Here the software is able to "learn" from its contact with the environment and change how it operates in response. The Internet sprang out of something called the World Wide Web, the design of which was very much affected by the concept of a spider's web and its inherent flexibility and strength.

GO DEEPER
Creative Systems: www.anthillsite.com

Room for More?

Developing our creativity and flexibility requires that we are open to the "new". This can be more challenging than it appears. If we are not open to new ways of doing things and, more importantly, new ways of seeing things, it is unlikely that we will be able to learn much. The following story told by Laurence Boldt, in his book *Zen and the Art of Making a Living* (p. 50), illustrates the pitfalls of not having room for new ideas.

A well-educated man once went to a Zen master to inquire about the meaning of Zen. After greeting him, the master instructed the visitor to be seated and proceeded to pour him a cup of tea. The cup was filled, and still he poured. Tea spilled over the sides of the table onto the floor, and still the Zen master poured. Finally, the visitor could contain himself no longer. "The cup is already full! It can hold no more!" The Zen master replied, "So it is. Just as you come to me so full of what you know that you can receive nothing new."

This story reminds me of an elderly in-law of my own, who used to insist he did not read the newspaper because "his mind was so full of stuff already" that he did not need any more. It should be no surprise that the gentleman in question was well known for his out-dated and inflexible ideas on most topics. He had inadvertently adopted the sea squirt strategy toward life.

D.I.Y. Creativity

Exercising our own personal creativity is an important first step toward developing our personal resilience. It also plays an important role in developing our CQ. By being flexible — and we can't be that without expressing our creativity — we are automatically open to opportunities for collaboration. As Robert Fritz puts it, "If you do not listen to your own being, you will have betrayed yourself."

Once we have accepted the idea that we have a creative self we will be able to express it more frequently. We will also be able to make a greater creative contribution to our team. When a team experiences this contribution, they then shift their perspective on us and come to rely more heavily upon our input. This forces us to tap into our creativity further and so it goes on.

What Can Creativity Achieve?

A story from the Oswego Valley Peace and Justice Council illustrates a very elegant application of a creative solution. An Indiana sheep farmer was concerned about the effect his neighbors' dogs were having on his sheep. Rather than resort to legal action or violence, the farmer gave his neighbors' children pet lambs as gifts. The neighbors then voluntarily tied up their dogs and even became close friends with the farmer. The act of searching for and finding creative solutions to problems could divide people and is also central to expanding our CQ.

Within the business environment there are a multitude of stories illustrating how fundamental creativity and flexibility is to the CQ of teams and organizations. The story of the 3M Corporation by now is legendary. Their Web site chronicles a century in which they became systematically more effective at applying creativity and innovation to practical problems. The result is a highly successful company and a foothold in many product areas.

As the world continues to change rapidly so companies and teams have to adapt to the changing environment. The Phillips Corporation is an example of a company that has embraced design as a guiding principle in this new "age of creativity". "It is not what you do — it is how you do it" could be the mantra of design specialists. As a result of Phillips taking the issue of design very seriously, 49% of their revenue for 2005 was from products introduced in the previous 12 months (the figure for 2003 was 25%). The preoccupation with design is just as pertinent to the design of our teams as it is to our products. Highly effective companies of the new era will be those that have put great thought into the design of their teams. CQ should be a major consideration for those of us involved in the creation and emancipation of functional teams.

WHERE WE'VE BEEN

A number of myths exists that can interfere with our ability to express our own creativity. In this chapter we explored these points:

- Creativity and flexibility is a central factor in all successful and sustainable teams.
- Innovation is creativity turned into practical action.
- Questions play an important role in stimulating our creativity.
- Creativity and innovation is not just important to the design of new products, but also to the design and emancipation of functional teams.

WHERE WE'RE GOING

With all the creativity and innovation in the world, if there is not an answer to the "why" question for teams to perform, chances are, effort will be minimal. Teams with high levels of CQ are not only creative, they also have a strong sense of purpose. This needs to make sense to the individual as well as the team. Each individual needs to be able to feel that they are participating meaningfully within their organization. This is the topic of the next chapter.

CQ Tool© 6

Developing Creative Capacity

There are three modes of thinking we tend to use when creating something or attempting to solve a problem. Walt Disney called these modes "Dreamer", "Realist", and "Critic".

The Dreamer mode is associated with ideas and thinking that makes no attempt to connect up with real life. The product of this mode of thinking tends to be very idealistic and can be impractical.

The Critic mode is associated with fault-finding and discovering the down-side of an idea or situation. The product of this thinking tends to be very pessimistic, and problem-focused.

The Realist mode is associated with a mixture of the Dreamer and Critic modes. The product of this mode of thinking tends to be idealism mixed with practical application and is often a workable and creative solution.

None of the modes are better than the others. They each have their strengths and weaknesses, so all are useful.

Walt Disney's strategy (which Dilts so cleverly spotted) is that during the creative or problem-solving process, all modes should be explored systematically.

Special thanks to Robert Dilts for allowing us to use this exercise from the Encyclopedia of Systemic Neuro-lingusitic Programming and NLP New Coding.

By spending time in each position we are able to disentangle the different types of thinking.

It was Disney's belief that each of these three elements needed to be represented in any creative process. It is reported that he often toured the various studios where films were being worked on and would spend time working out if any of the rooms were missing one of the modes. When he spotted a lack of dreamer or critic, he would take on that role and become engaged in the creative process with that particular team. His behavior provides us a great example of someone who has expanded his behavioral flexibility to the degree of becoming what the team needs at any particular time.

One of the signs of teams with high CQ is that its members are able and willing to express that aspect of themselves (including a mode of thinking) that best serves the team's objective.

STEP 1: Create three physical locations for the three modes of thinking. This can be achieved by placing three pieces of paper on the floor labeled "Dreamer", "Realist", and "Critic".

STEP 2: Establish modes of thinking for the Dreamer location. Go to the Dreamer location and think of a time when you were very creative in a very uninhibited way. Assume a physical state of relaxation and evenly balanced body position, with your eyes looking up. This physical state becomes anchored to the dreamer location.

STEP 3: Establish modes of thinking for the Critic location. Go to the Critic location and think of a time when you were able to constructively criticize a plan or idea. The physical state you assume is of an angular posture, for example one hand to your chin with eyes down and head tilted down. This physical state becomes anchored to the Critic location.

STEP 4: Establish modes of thinking for the Realist location. Go to the Realist location and think of a time when you were able to realistically assess a plan or idea and put them effectively into action. The physical state you assume is of a balanced posture, eyes and head pointed straight ahead, hands on hips as if you were ready to take action. This physical state becomes anchored to the Realist location.

STEP 5: Choose an outcome you wish to achieve and step into the Dreamer location. Create an image of yourself achieving that goal, almost as if you were a character in a movie. If you notice a critical voice beginning to surface in your mind, simply switch it off and remind yourself that this is the Dreamer location and that you will visit the Critic presently.

STEP 6: Repeat Step 5 with the Critic and Realist locations, each time shaking off the effects of each of those modes of thinking. Note thoughts that come up from each of the locations. Criticisms should be turned into questions that can be explored from the dreamer location.

STEP 7: After cycling through the three locations several times you may wish to end by going to the realist location and assembling a plan of action based upon all the things you have discovered about the desired goal.

The difference this process makes is that you focus on one type of thinking at a time. If you discover critical thoughts arising while you are in the dreamer space you can do a couple of things. You can step out of the dreamer space and step into the critic space, or you can adjust your thinking back to dreamer. A very useful development of this exercise involves creating a dialogue between the different spaces (you switching between spaces while exploring the different perspectives and vocalizing their perspectives).

Meaningful Participation

*Do more than belong: participate. Do more
than care: help. Do more than believe: practice.
Do more than be fair: be kind. Do more than
forgive: forget. Do more than dream: work.*

WILLIAM ARTHUR WARD

Everyone I know likes to think that what they are doing matters
and that their contribution to life makes a difference. This is the
essence of meaningful participation — making a difference. By definition collaborative intelligence involves meaningful participation.
Intelligence that emerges as a result of collaboration must involve
participation. The "meaningful" part comes in, of course, when the
participants are aware that their contribution matters and is important to the system as a whole. The challenge comes when we try to

achieve meaningful participation everyday. In the flurry of getting things done and meeting deadlines, it is easy to lose sight of the big picture. This goes on until we become exhausted and begin to wonder, "what's the point of all this?" At this time it is useful to stop and ask ourselves, "What am I assuming about my part in the system?"

> *The only happy people I know are the ones who are working well at something they consider important.*
> ABRAHAM MASLOW

Assumptions About Participation

The very first skill we explored in this book was assumptions. In many ways, we have come full circle. Meaningful participation is one of the most powerful assumptions you can make. To assume that your life has meaning has many implications, just as the opposite would have.

Another assumption that has a very specific (and limiting) effect is that there is a "reality" out there to be discovered. Like a school exam, we are then faced with the task of finding the right answer; finding out as much about it as possible.

Nietzsche said that people can "survive any *how* if they have a sufficient *why*". We know that when we attach a great deal of meaning to something, like the outcome of a football game or our child's first word, we get very excited and absorbed in the event. The same is true of our work. When we have a strong sense of meaning attached to what we are doing, we bring more of our attention and energy to it. Sadly, many people have been so disillusioned by their experience of work and, beyond a paycheck, they have stripped it of all meaning. This is one of the reasons volunteer work is so rewarding. As a volunteer we have chosen to discover rewards beyond monetary gain. We feel as if we have made a difference and attach meaning to that contribution. Something special goes on — meaning is being made.

What Have We Chosen Our Work to Mean?

Notice that this question assumes that we can choose meaning. One of the things that we so frequently forget is that we do have choice. It is easy to become distracted by the number of things in which we have no choice. Viktor Frankl took this observation to its logical conclusion and discovered that we are the meaning makers and that ultimately we define our lives by the meanings we choose to adopt. If we wish to change our lives, Frankl advocates that we examine closely the meanings we have assigned to the various parts of our lives.

There is an old story about a man who came upon three stonemasons — each carving a piece of stone. When asked what he was doing, the first man replied he was "earning enough money to feed his children". The second said he was, "applying his art to the best of his ability". The third said he was, "building a cathedral". All of the men had the same job — the meaning they applied was quite different.

We are fortunate that we live in a society where we can ask the question, "What is meaningful participation at work and how can I find it for myself?" The dynamic between freedom and responsibility emerges here again — with the freedom to ask such questions comes the responsibility to ask the other questions, such as "What are we here for?" — and eventually — "Can I make a difference?" The faint of heart may step back from asking that question, which is one of the reasons we talk about courage in this chapter.

"Generation Y" is creating an impact upon the way we organize ourselves at work. One of the defining characteristics of this very large cohort (second only to Baby Boomers) is their concern that the company they work for has values that match their own. Also they need to understand how their work contributes to the organization's bottom line. In short, Gen Y needs to know they can make a difference; meaningful participation is extremely important to them.

Saying Yes

> *This is the true joy in life, the being used for a purpose recognized by yourself as a mighty one; the being thoroughly worn out before you are thrown on the scrap heap; the being a force of Nature instead of a feverish selfish little clod of ailments and grievances complaining that the world will not devote itself to making you happy.*
> GEORGE BERNARD SHAW, *MAN AND SUPERMAN*, EPISTLE DEDICATORY

The whole idea of meaningful participation can be a little overwhelming. I am not suggesting that in order for teams to achieve it they must make some heroic gesture. We all start where we are and work out from there. Small is good. Small enables us not to be discouraged by the thought of how much there is to be done and how important it is.

To become the force of nature that Shaw talks about does not necessarily mean all our actions must be grand gestures. First steps are often small, and initial visions that focus energy effectively often address immediate problems. What matters is engagement in the service of a larger purpose rather than lofty aspirations that paralyze action. This becomes even more important when we consider teams. The team can provide a context for the individual members, in the same way that a department provides a context to the team. On the macro level the organization is providing a context to all its groups, divisions, and teams. This is why the values that an organization embraces become so important; they create a context for the activities of everyone who works there. Increasingly employees want to know if their employer operates a "triple bottom line" (financial, social, and environmental considerations with respect to business planning). As people become more systemically aware, they want to know if their company is having an adverse or beneficial effect upon the community and environment.

> *What matters is engagement in the service of a larger purpose rather than lofty aspirations that paralyze action.*

Courage Under Fire

The scene in *Oliver Twist*, in which Oliver goes back to ask for more porridge, reveals the courage he displayed in the face of unknown consequences. To me the request for more is symbolic not of greed but of saying, "I need more and am willing to ask the question". It could also represent asking to have more meaning. Too often we have learned to keep our heads down, not asking the tricky questions.

Earlier in the book I spoke about the possible transformation effects of asking good questions. In this case it could be, "What is the deeper meaning of my work?" or "What could my work mean?"

It is said that the Red Sea did not part for Moses until Naashon had waded into the water up to his nose. What better way to demonstrate our own inner leadership than to be willing to wade into the water up to our noses? True courage is never a calculation of risk, a quadratic equation of factors determining what we do — it is a commitment to what needs to be done irrespective of the cost or risk.

Deciding to have meaningful participation in our work will eventually test our courage. A famous bull fighter was once asked to define courage. He said that to step into a ring when you are not afraid is nothing. To not step into a ring when you are afraid is also nothing. To step into the ring when you are afraid, now that is something, he added. Sometimes the most fear is associated with doing the right thing and tests our dedication to the 'higher path'.

> *True courage is never a calculation of risk — it is a commitment to what needs to be done irrespective of the cost or risk.*

Work as Contribution

Juanita Brown in *World Café* says, "Contribution has a different tone and feeling than individual participation. Important as it is, the focus on individual participation can lead to an overemphasis on the I: I'm voicing my opinions. I'm speaking up. I'm participating. In contrast, focusing on contribution creates a relationship between the I and the we."

GO DEEPER
Contribution: www.anthillsite.com

I think this makes a beautiful point about the connection between ourselves and the teams we are on. We are required to let go of ego to make this type of contribution possible. When we can contribute rather than participate, our team benefits by having a model of what contribution is really about — that is, serving the team and its purpose first, rather than our own ego needs.

For most of us, what we do for a living has become an extension of who we are as a person. Eight plus hours per day, five days per week is a lot of life tied up in something. I am reminded of the cartoon of the man lying on his death bed, his family around him, and he shares with them, "I watched a lot of TV, ate a lot of junk food, and sold more ceramic tiles in May of 1998 than anyone else in the northern region. My work here is done." What will we be able to say on our death beds? Sobering question.

The argument is that most of us spend too much time at work for it to have no meaning at all. Helping people to see the part their contribution plays in the grander scheme of things enables them to get the best out of themselves. This goes for teams as well. A good team leader (whether they have been asked to or not) connects the dots for the team members in terms of the larger organizational objectives. Among other things this provides a context for requests around performance. For example if I needed to ask a team to work a portion of the weekend, it helps to make sense of this request if I explain that the department needs the work completed because of an audit that is being carried out the following week.

I am sure we have all had to do something like this and such requests can have varying results. The difference in the responses we receive has less to do with the kind of request and more with whether the team members feel as committed to the organization as they are to the team. When the organization is striving to do something with which the individual can identify and support, then commitment (instead of compliance) is much more likely.

Freiberg's heroic causes show how companies can help employees connect with the larger purpose of what they are doing. For example, when Apple says, "We want to educate the world" they are effectively saying people who work for us can say, "I work for a company that is in the business of educating the world" — a lofty ambition indeed. Even the character in the cartoon (the ceramic tile salesman) could have said, "I help people create clean and hygienic homes for their families to grow up in," if he had chosen to view it that way.

The Most Difficult Question of All

The most important questions in life also tend to be the most challenging — the question of purpose is no exception. Pema Chodron, in Brach's *Radical Acceptance*, relates the story of a lady who sat next to her mother as she lay unconscious, close to death. One morning the dying mother opened her eyes and looked in her daughter's eyes and said, "You know, all my life I thought something was wrong with me." She then shook her head as if to say, "What a waste." The mother then closed her eyes and died shortly after. None of us wish to reach this point where we are viewing our whole life as a waste. This makes meaningful participation the most important issues, not only from a personal perspective but also from a professional one.

My wife once accused me of being a little morbid because I liked to read the obituaries. In my defense I explained that I enjoyed reading what those closest to them, thought about them and the life they led. Beyond the devoted father, committed Christian, and faithful friend, there are often singular and surprising comments that provide an insight into the real impact the deceased possessed, when alive. Beyond the clichés these latter comments often indicate how the person engaged with life.

> *When we are born, we are crying and everyone*
> *around us is smiling. When we die, may we be*
> *smiling while everyone around us is crying.*
> JEWISH PROVERB

In many workshops I ask at the beginning for participants to identify a personal hero. When sharing with the group, it is surprising the number of people who have chosen their mother, father, grandmother, or an old high school teacher. Many of the heroes are deceased and continue to have a deep impact upon our lives. If the people are no longer physically around, what is it that continues to affect us? Often as not, it is the values they championed, values that we ourselves wish to honor. And yet we are all a work in progress and every moment is another opportunity to ask the question, "How can I participate more meaningfully in my work?" or "How can I honor the values that matter to me in my work?"

Finding Meaning at Work

One hundred years ago it would have seemed absurd to write about people's need to find meaning in their work. In the early 1900s a very small proportion of the population of the world were aware of the value of meaningful work. For everyone else work was only a means of feeding themselves and their family. The industrial revolution created a world in which people were cogs in a giant machine. Society, in first world countries, is emerging from the industrial age to the information age. There are the beginnings of a knowledge or creativity age appearing beyond that. These layers of development can be viewed as levels of evolution. As William Gibson said once, "The future is already here, it's just unevenly distributed."

We live on a planet where there are people still living in near-stone-age conditions (e.g., the isolated aboriginals of Australia) and where probes are being sent to explore Pluto.

For those of you wishing to explore a model that explains the different levels of society and the process of their evolution, refer to the *Spiral Dynamics Model* (Beck and Cowen, 1998) and the book *A Theory of Everything* (Wilber, 1996).

GO DEEPER
Human Society Evolves: www.anthillsite.com

It is impossible to explore the topic of collaborative intelligence and resilience properly, without bumping into the issue of meaning. I expect that you are no different from the majority of the population — you want your life to have meaning and to have it make a difference. If you are to spend on average 20,000 hours of your life at work over the next ten years then does it not make sense to want what you do to contribute to that sense of "making a difference" (the odd hours of voluntary work outside of it hardly makes a splash in comparison). Maslow mentions this connection to a cause when he refers to, "An easy medicine for self-esteem: becomes a part of something important. …This identification with important causes, or important jobs, this identifying with them and taking them into the self thereby enlarging the self and making it important, this is a way of over coming also actual existential human shortcomings e.g. IQ, talent, abilities etc."

Holding Our Lives

Like each strand of the spider's web, each life is an integral part of the whole. Though at some level it is indistinguishable from all the rest. The paradox of individualism and collectivism is resolved not by choosing one of them as an option, but by realizing that they are a dynamic (just like freedom and responsibility) and a dynamic is lived rather than resolved.

> *Like each strand of the spider's web, each life is an integral part of the whole.*

Errol Flynn, the 50s Hollywood actor, got his start in the movies as a stunt man — he had been an Olympic fencer prior to that. A journalist once asked him to reveal the secret of being a great fencer. Flynn's reply bears some contemplation. He said that it all depended on how you held the sword. If you held it too tightly your movements would be stiff and predictable and you would be beaten. On the other hand if you held it too loosely, it would be knocked from your hand by your opponent. When pressed to explain how would he know how tightly to hold it, Flynn simply explained that depended on what was going on in the moment.

How tightly do you need to hold onto your life? Too loosely and it will be knocked from your hands — it will become part of someone else's plan. Too tightly and your life becomes a stiff and predictable dance destined to leave you feeling that somehow life walked right past you.

One thing seems to be pretty consistent — the universe has a strange and subtle sense of balance — you get back what you put in. Your "outer life" (as much as you would like to believe otherwise) is a mirror of what is going on with the "inner life". This is the first furrow; this is where personal development meets professional development — you are not two people — the one with the brief case and the one with the golf club in your hand. Laurence Boldt talks about the illusion of the balance between work and life as if they were the opposites of each other. If we choose to perceive them as such so shall it be and never the twain will meet. What a waste I say, what a crying shame that each time you go off to the office you bring just some part of you to the activity and leave another part behind.

Work can be (as I'm sure it is for some of you already) another way for us to express ourselves. If it is not, we are technically not different from being a slave. Never have human beings had more choice; never has the call to live our authentic life been easier to hear. It hasn't got any easier to answer the call. The call will always be challenging to respond to, always have appreciable costs, and always frighten us.

Courage Under Fire

The question of courage always appears when we begin to factor in the costs of meaningful participation. True courage is never a calculation of risk, a quadratic equation of factors determining what we do — it is a commitment to what needs to be done irrespective of the cost or risk. Deciding to have meaningful participation in our work will eventually test our courage. A story from Viktor Frankl's *The Unheard Cry For Meaning* provides us with a way of thinking about the courage required (p. 53).

"During World War I a Jewish army doctor was sitting together with his gentile friend, an aristocratic colonel, in a foxhole when heavy shooting began. Teasingly, the colonel said, 'You are afraid, aren't you? Just another proof that the Aryan race is superior to the Semitic one.' 'Sure, I am afraid,' was the doctor's answer. 'But who is superior? If you, my dear colonel, were as afraid as I am. You would have run away long ago.' What counts are not our fears and anxieties as such, but the attitude we adopt toward them. This attitude is freely chosen."

Practically every single major contribution humans have made to life was through some aspect of what could have been called "work" — Michael Angelo and his art; Madame Curie and her science; Schweitzer and his medicine; and Martin Luther King, Jr. and his politics. These people could be perceived as driven, however I'm sure they would have still done what they did even if they thought their work might go unnoticed. They did it because it was an expression of who they were. Everyone's life (including the work part) can be an expression of who they are.

"A Hammer, a Hammer, my Kingdom for a Hammer"

We don't need any more tools, we have piles of them. In *Stewardship*, Peter Block once counted how many suggestions were made for how people could improve their working life within just four books — *Thriving on Chaos*, *Seven Habits of Highly Effective People*, *The Empowered Manager*, and *The Fifth Discipline*. He came up with 925 suggestions about how people could make positive changes to their workplace. Block's conclusion to this observation was that "how" was not the question that needed to be asked — we are awash in "how-tos". The question is, "What will it take for you to take the next step; to embrace the challenge?" Life requires us to look inside and say "yes" to the challenge. We are drowning in strategies, processes and tools; what we need is commitment.

Swallow or Be Swallowed

When I was seven, my parents bought me the Larousse *Animal Life Encyclopedia*. In it I found the most gruesome picture I had ever seen. It was two Egyptian Vipers; each had bitten opposite ends of a single rat. The commentary beside the picture explained that because Egyptian Viper's fangs are permanently angled backwards, once they have seized their prey they can never let go — they are committed to swallow whatever they bite. I immediately became very curious what was going to happen in this situation — an Egyptian Viper committed to opposite ends of the same prey. The commentary went on to explain that one of the vipers would have to swallow the rat and then the other viper. I realize that this is a pretty gruesome story, but I think that our own lives are no less dramatic and the stakes no less considerable.

To have meaningful participation we must be committed. Stop and think about the word for a few moments and what it means to the snake as it strikes its prey, knowing that its fangs are angled backwards. Once impaled upon its prey, it is committed, there is no letting go, no dropping the idea, no "I'll let this one go and take the next one", no way out. Sounds so final, drastic.

An example of this level of commitment can be found in Mahatma Gandhis battle with the British Empire. Gandhi would never let go, even though his only "weapons" were intent, love, and a philosophy of non-violence.

If we do not fully live our lives then who will live them? The cliché of having our children live out our aspirations is a cul de sac at the very least and more commonly, disastrous for everyone involved. No matter what our parents taught us — we now know that our lives are our responsibility. What we say "yes" to will shape our lives for ever, just as what we are saying "no" to right now is shaping it. If we stand still and ask "how" forever, then that is a choice, though one that will probably not bring us what we seek.

Saying "yes" does not necessarily take away the pain, but gives it, and our lives, a richer meaning.

> *If we do not fully live our lives then who will live them?*

Peter Block quotes Sister DeShano (the director of a large health care system he worked with). She said, "the call comes from a place that we do not know, that the demands placed on us will be more than we ever expected, and that if we knew what was in store, we never would have said yes. These are excellent tests for the pursuit of what matters." The "call" she is referring to was, of course, the call to participate meaningfully in her life and her work.

The Magic of Action

Many people have reached this crossroads in their life. You may have already reached it. When we take that step over the line and commit ourselves, something special happens. W. H. Murray of the Scottish Himalayan Expedition in 1951 put it this way:

"Concerning all acts of initiative (and creation) there is one elementary truth, the ignorance of which kills countless ideas and splendid plans: that the moment one definitely commits oneself, then providence moves too. All sorts of things occur to help one that would not otherwise have occurred. A wild stream of events issues from the decision, raising in one's favor all manner of unforeseen incidents and meetings and material assistance which no man would have dreamed would come his way. I have learned a deep respect for one of Goethe's couplets: 'Whatever you can do, or dream you can, begin it. Boldness had genius, magic, and power in it. Begin it now.'"

Rationalizations are described by Steven Pressfield in *The War of Art* as the right-hand man of resistance. The person who coined the phrase "resistance is useless" obviously hadn't thought it through. Resistance is very useful — it prevents us from doing a great many things that require commitment. It stops us short of achieving great things many times. It tells us "it's not worth the bother" and saves us from disappointments in life. It saves us the trouble of discovering deeper levels of our own resiliency.

Meaningful Participation Means Creating the Future

To be a meaningful participant is to realize that we are creating the future moment–by–moment through what we choose to say "yes" to. When I think of this important aspect of meaningful participation I remember a story from Paul Rogat Loeb's book, *The Impossible Will Take a Little Longer.*

Rogat Loeb relates a true incident in the life of surrealist poet, Robert Desnos, during the Second World War. He was being taken, with a truck load of other prisoners, to be gassed. Everyone on the truck knew where they were going and there was a dreadful silence as they disembarked beside the gas chambers. Suddenly Desnos stepped into the line and grabbed another prisoner's hand and began to read his palm. He foresaw many children and much good luck. Soon many others were reaching out their palms to have them read. Each time the story was similar — long life, abundant joy, and many children. By that time the mood among the prisoners and the guards had changed — whether they were so disorientated or moved by the unfolding scene — the guards became unable to follow their orders and simply loaded the prisoners back into the truck and drove them back to the camp. Desnos had saved the lives of everyone by creating an almost absurd but contagious prediction of the future.

By choosing to *see* something different Desnos was able to carry the imaginations of his fellow prisoners and even the guards to a new place and the result — the creation of a miracle. The frightening and beautiful truth is that each moment we live, we can ask the "what if" question. What if my work or the work of my team could be meaningful?

On Hope and Fear

In Buddhist philosophy hope is not the opposite of hopelessness — fear is. Vacal Havel once stated, "Hope is not the conviction that something will turn out well, but the certainty

> *If we do not fill our hearts with hope then fear will rush in to fill the space.*

that something makes sense regardless of how it turns out."

Nature abhors a vacuum and if we do not fill our hearts with hope then fear will rush in to fill the space. It's our choice.

How Real is Real?

At work, it can be so easy to assume we have to be a certain type of person to be accepted and make progress within the team and organization. It is so tempting to put on our game face each time we enter the workplace. Palmer J. Parker relates an old Hasidic tale that reveals, with amazing brevity, both the universal tendency to want to be someone else and the ultimate importance of becoming one's self. Rabbi Zusya, when he was an old man, said, "In the coming world, they will not ask me: 'Why were you not Moses?' They will ask me: 'Why were you not Zusya?'"

I used to work with a colleague who often joked that 80% of success was showing up, an old Woody Allen joke. In the morning, when he had arrived at the office, he would say, "Well that's 80% of my work done for the day." I am quite sure he was unaware of another meaning for the term "showing up". This second meaning relates to the act of bringing our true selves to work. This enables us to be more authentic with those around us. After all, 20,000 hours over the next ten years is a long time to be playing a part. Like any other attribute, it grows as it is exercised.

> *"What is REAL?" asked the Rabbit one day, when they were lying side by side.... "Does it mean having things — that buzz inside you and a stick-out-handle?"*
>
> *"Real isn't how you are made," said the Skin Horse. "It's a thing that happens to you. When a child loves you for a long, long time, not just to play with, but REALLY loves, you, then you become real."*
>
> *"Does it hurt?" asked the Rabbit.*
>
> *"Sometimes," said the Skin Horse, for he was always truthful. "When you are real you don't mind being hurt."*
>
> *"Does it happen all at once, like being wound up," he asked, "or bit by bit?"*
>
> *"It doesn't happen all at once," said the Skin Horse. "You become. It takes a long time. That's why it doesn't often happen to people who break easily, or have sharp edges, or who have to be carefully*

kept. Generally, by the time you are real, most of your hair has been loved off, and your eyes drop out and you get loose in the joints and very shabby. But these things don't matter at all, because once you are Real you can't be ugly, except to people who don't understand."
MARGERY WILLIAMS, *THE VELVETEEN RABBIT*

Being "real" in the professional arena is not always easy. More and more people want their work to be an extension of their life, an expression of who they are, rather than an uncomfortable appendage that they must accommodate. For these people meaningful participation is a vital ingredient of the work experience. Forward thinking and evolved organizations will increasingly champion opportunities for building meaning into how they function. This will, in turn, enable employees to bring all of themselves to their professional roles. The end result? Employees, teams, and organizations sharing a sense of aligned purpose that brings forth their collaborative intelligence in a meaningful way.

WHERE WE'VE BEEN

- We need leaders to support us, as we strive to live and work by our values.
- "Why" is an important question when it comes to how we relate to our work.
- We are the meaning makers and ultimately we decide the meaning of our work.
- Being personally authentic is an important part of discovering meaningful participation at work.
- Discovering meaningful participation will often test our courage.

- Building a sense of meaningful participation within teams automatically builds CQ.
- Companies that champion meaningful participation will attract the employees best equipped to take the company into the future.

 ## WHERE WE'RE GOING

The skills we have explored so far have been designed to help develop the CQ of individuals and teams. We have also touched upon the topic of resilience throughout the book. Building resilient teams is an important way to develop the collaborative intelligence of organizations. The next chapter explores this topic.

CQ Tool© 7

Exploring Values to Discover Meaning

Values can act as a compass to provide us direction through-out our lives. When life becomes turbulent or we sail through foggy weather, it is useful to have our values close at hand to help us navigate.

STEP 1: On a separate sheet of paper recall a time when

- You have been most creative;
- You have been most committed to something;
- You have made your mind up to do something (despite people telling you couldn't do it) and did it despite all the obstacles; and
- You have been so absorbed in something that you ceased to notice time passing.

Take a few moments for each question and jot down some notes about what comes to mind.

STEP 2: For each of the instances that come to mind, determine the value being suggested. What was it that was motivating you to do what you were doing? Write down your answers.

Note: To get the juices flowing you may want to Google values; you will find many sites displaying long lists of values.

STEP 3: You should be able to spot some values that have emerged from this exercise. Place them in order of priority.

STEP 4: Ask yourself, "How can I honor these values in my work place?" or "If I were honoring these values in my day-to-day work, what would that look like?"

Note: Your team might like to explore this exercise together. It could help to bring team members to a deeper understanding of the values that are important to their colleagues. This can lead to the next step — a shared set of values for the whole team.

You have now taken some simple steps towards identifying how to bring more meaningful participation into your work life.

Building High CQ Teams

*Experience is a hard teacher because she gives
the test first, the lesson afterwards.*

VERNON LAW

So what does a team with high CQ look like? Is it a spectacular sight that takes your breath away when you see it in action? Like the Cirque de Soliel, would it baffle and mesmerize the audience with its death-defying feats? Not really. Such teams metaphorically appear more like a flock of starlings at twilight. As you look at the flock you may recognize it as a group of individuals; however, it seems as if they are informed by the one group mind, as they twist and turn, adapting to their environment. It's difficult to make out who the leader is and yet the group as a whole behaves in a purposeful and effective fashion. Each member of the flock/team has their own freedom of action and takes every chance it gets to choreograph its flight with that of the flock.

Collaboratively Intelligent Teams Are Boring

It could be said that teams with high CQ are quite boring. There are very few dramas and no exciting heroes the team relies on to save the day. People pull their weight and support each other to an extraordinary degree. There is a vigorous pursuit for learning, not only at the individual level, but at the team level also. There is a sense of community within the team or department. People from outside sense this very quickly and notice something special is going on. We have all had this experience and most of us can't put our finger on what it is. Like the difference between listening to a well-rehearsed orchestra and a group of novice musicians that are playing out of key.

> *A team with high CQ expects challenge and meets it with one eye on results; the other on what it can learn from each encounter.*

A team with high CQ expects challenge and meets it with one eye on results and the other on what it can learn from each encounter with something new.

A collaboratively intelligent team realizes that all great teams are a process, not a thing. This is based upon strong bonds between its members. There is an awareness that *each person* in the team is also a process and not static. Personality profiles are perceived as general guides but each person is encouraged to grow and change in positive ways. Team members know that a great deal of behavior is determined by the situation and they consciously create situations where collaboration is easy and fruitful. The assumption is that no matter what the personality of the team member, there will always be opportunities for high levels of collaboration.

The purpose of this book was not to make you and your team boring — there are others benefits of building high CQ teams.

- A High CQ team is able to *share the stress and strain* evenly throughout the team — like a tennis racket takes the impact of a ball at one point in the racket and the pressure is spread throughout all the strings.
- A High CQ team has a strong network of connection and support between its members. This *accelerates learning* enabling the team's reactions to be rapid and responsive to the challenges the team encounters.
- A High CQ team looks after its own; individuals are not left to fend for themselves and *staff retention is high* because people feel a strong sense of belonging.
- A High CQ team is well connected with other teams and with corporate objectives. Like a healthy organ in the body — it *knows what its function is and serves the greater good* through rough times and smooth.
- A high CQ team *achieves its objectives more through people* and less through politics
- A High CQ team replenishes itself, growing its members, and is constantly *learning to better adapt to its environment.*
- A high CQ team displays *a strong sense of meaningful participation*, which the members are all nourished by.

So teams with High CQ are already out there and as the importance of collaborative intelligence becomes more recognized, more will emerge. Other factors are at work within this mix, however. There is a "changing of the guard" within businesses, most noticeably in those countries with large baby boomer populations.

Y are They Important?

As the baby boomers begin to leave the stage another generation begins to makes its presence more obvious — generation "Y". North Americans born between 1977 and 2003 make up this generation. "Gen Y" is the second largest cohort after the baby boomers and while much more varied in their characteristics, these cohorts may share many of their values. Asked what their three most important values were when choosing a company to work for, they choose integrity, social responsibility, and loyalty. Asked what they valued most about their work and Gen Y quickly isolated teamwork, work-life balance, stimulating work, and lots of feedback. Honoring these values in the workplace, we will build businesses that will help the Gen Y's become and remain engaged. Gen Y is also much more multicultural than the baby boomer cohort and so training in the area of diversity will help in the process of developing high CQ teams.

The shifting generations are having a huge effect upon how business can work through teams. As Gen Y begins to infuse the workforce with different values and perspectives, we will have to find a way to accommodate their arrival and prepare for the departure of the baby boomers.

Mentoring and coaching will become more important as a way to effectively transfer all the soft information and skills between the generations within the business environment. Other management strategies to assist Gen Y in the process of taking over the reins include:

- providing training in time management;
- offering community involvement opportunities;
- creating a system for frequent public praise for performance;
- creating many opportunities for team involvement; and
- customizing the career paths for employees.

GO DEEPER
Gen Y and Baby Boomers: www.anthillsite.com

Knowledge management is clearly an issue here. Valuable information the baby boomers are carrying around with them needs to be transferred across to their Gen Y colleagues. For these reasons we have chosen multi-dimensional coaching as the CQ Tool© for this chapter. This tool enables coaching to occur in many directions.

Multi-Dimensional Coaching

With fewer layers of management, employees must assume greater responsibility (with the support of their management team) in taking initiative and sharing in the leadership process. The most resilient companies will be those through which leadership flows. Leadership in such companies will become a fluid process that touches every one at every level.

> *Every employee must be willing to lead and be lead.*

Every employee must be willing to lead and be lead. A different way of relating to others is required to make the shift from *depending on others* to *contributing through others*. Team members who are contributing through others will have the ability to:

- develop technical breadth;
- broaden business perspective;
- stimulate others with ideas and knowledge;
- be involved as a leader, mentor or idea-generator in developing others; and
- build strong networks (internal and external).

Teaching an Anthill to Coach

Developing the CQ of teams requires that we look closely at how we interact with each other. One of the most effective ways to accomplish this task is by developing team members' ability to coach each other. Coaching develops the team's ability to learn from and contribute through each other. It is a central strategy of a flattened organization. Coaching can be directed in three main ways as demonstrated in Figure 8.1.

Figure 8.1
Multi-Dimensional Coaching

We refer to this approach as "multi-dimensional". Organizational structure and management accountability taken to one side, the actual process of performance coaching consists of essentially the same process whichever direction it is conducted. A coach is someone that helps others with the tools, knowledge, and opportunities they need to develop themselves and become more effective.

Coaches don't develop others — they help others develop themselves. By definition, then, most employees have the potential to be effective coaches in all three directions. Informal coaching processes offer tremendous potential for releasing untapped energy from teams. With informal coaching comes the prospect of every employee becoming involved in the organization's growth and development. This makes multi-dimensional coaching an important CQ Tool© in the development of CQ within teams.

CQ Tools© 8

The LEADing Change System©

The LEAD System© represents a simple coaching method that can be used in any of the three coaching directions. The acronym ensures that important elements are addressed during each coaching conversation.

The system consists of four stages:

- **Leverage**
- **Environment**
- **Alternatives**
- **Development**

We can also represent this system in a diagram.

LEADing Change

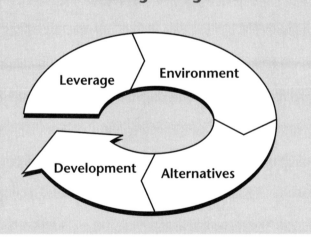

Leverage is the point of entry and represents the opportunity for change. It may be discovered when someone says something about a change they would like to make in their effectiveness or something with which they are unhappy. For all intentional purposes it represents the *goal* of the coaching session. The leverage stage achieves the following:

- discovers a topic for discussion;
- explores the reason for desired change;
- establishes an objective for the coaching conversation; and
- creates a long-term goal when appropriate.

Environment represents the present reality. This includes a description of what is presently happening. Jim Collins would describe this stage as the "brutal facts". It may include behaviors (including those of other people involved) and a description of the situation that lead to the "leverage point". The environment stage achieves the following:

- encourages self-assessment;
- provides an appreciative feedback sandwich;
- surfaces assumptions; and
- discounts immaterial history.

Alternatives represent the range of choices available for making changes. It may involve imagining the ideal future or brainstorming paths forward. Assumptions have such a strong impact on our lives; this stage can be a second chance to evaluate any assumptions that may affect the generation of alternatives. This stage achieves the following:

- explores the full range of alternatives;
- brainstorms with coachee around ways forward;
- carefully offers suggestions; and
- coaches them to a choice.

Development represents the point at which the coachee prepares to take action. This is also the place that the coachee identifies how and where they will make changes. The LEAD system is a cyclical process and the final stage is really a connection to revisiting the leverage stage. By doing this the coach and coachee are able to have another conversation around the coaching issue. However this time around the issue has been (all being well) moved forward by the coachee. If necessary the LEAD process can help the coachee make further progress. The development stage achieves the following:

- gains commitment from the coachee to take action;
- anticipates potential obstacles;
- creates specific timelines and plans for next step; and
- provides support for change process.

Use the LEADing Change diagram in this exercise to guide the process. Start with low risk issues to practice with the system. Arrange to have follow-up sessions with the person you are working. This can be achieved by saying you would be interested in hearing how they got on with the next step.

So Where Are We Going...

Can you teach an anthill to fetch? It depends on how you define "fetch". If we are using the term as a metaphor for enabling a large number of individuals to achieve an unprecedented level of coordination, then yes it is possible to teach an anthill to fetch. This book has been an exploration of the principles and processes that make that possible for teams and organizations.

In this hyper-linked world, harnessing the attention and energy of a team has never been more challenging. IQ and EQ (Emotional Intelligence) are necessary but no longer sufficient to deal with the present rate of change. Getting people onboard and keeping them there demands a new level of collaboration.

Teaching an anthill to fetch is a metaphor. A metaphor for all the things we know our team could do. Moving a group of people from one way of operating to another is very like teaching an anthill to fetch. Given the right approach to the challenge and the right tools, we can develop the CQ of our teams and organizations.

The Collaborative Intelligence of a team is defined as the capacity to create, contribute to, and harness the intelligence within the group. By raising the level of CQ everyone benefits. This unique combination of practical CQ Tools© and processes helps teams to:

- attract and retain high quality team members;
- create a sense of meaningful participation;
- collaborate in highly effective ways;
- connect to a strong sense of purpose; and
- balance leadership and followship.

Developing CQ enables teams to build strong connections and tap into the awe-inspiring power within each of us. It also helps teams realize that none of us is as intelligent as all of us.

Good teams and organizations have developed good levels of CQ; great ones have great CQ. There has never been a more opportune moment in time to decide to do something — for our teams, our employees, our organizations, and ourselves.

Bibliography

Beck, Don Edward and Christopher Cowan. *Spiral Dynamics: Mastering Values, Leadership and Change* (reprint). Blackwell Publishing, Incorporated, 2005

Block, Peter. *Stewardship.* Berrett-Koehler, 1996

Block, Peter. *The Answer to How Is Yes: Acting on What Matters.* Berrett-Koehler Publishers, 2003

Block, Peter. *The Empowered Manager: Positive Political Skills at Work.* Jossey-Bass, 1991

Bloom, Howard. Global *Brain: The Evolution of Mass Mind from the Big Bang to the 21st Century.* Wiley, 2000

Boldt, Laurence. *Zen and the Art of Making a Living: A Practical Guide to Creative Career Design.* Penguin (Non-Classics), 1999

Brach, Tara. *Radical Acceptance.* Bantam, 2004

Brown, Juanita with David Isaacs and the World Café Community. *The World Café: Shaping Our Futures Through Conversations That Matter.* Berrett-Koehler Publishers, 2005

Buckingham, Marcus and Donald O. Clifton. *Now, Discover Your Strengths.* Pocket Books, 2005

Capra, Fritjof. *The Web of Life: A New Scientific Understanding of Living Systems.* Anchor, 1997

Carroll, Lewis. *Alice Through the Looking Glass.* Gramercy, 2004

Childre, Doc Lew and Bruce Cryer. *From Chaos to Coherence (The Power to Change Performance).* HeartMath, 2000

Collins, Jim. *Good to Great: Why Some Companies Make the Leap... and Others Don't.* Harper Collins, 2001

Covey, Stephen R. *The 7 Habits of Highly Effective People,* 15th anniversay edition. Free Press, 2004

Csikszentmihalyi, Mihaly. *Flow the Psychology of Optimal Experience.* HarperCollins Publisher, 1990

Dilts, Robert. *Encyclopedia of Systemic Neuro-Linguistic Programming and NLP New Coding.* N L P University Press, 2000

Eidser, John. *Global Brain: The Evolution of Mass Mind from the Big Bang to the 21st Century.* Wiley, 2001

Flemons, Douglas G. *Completing Distinctions: Interweaving the Ideas of Gregory Bateson and Taoism into a unique approach to therapy.* Shambhala, 2001

Frankl, Viktor E. *Man's Search for Meaning.* Beacon Press, 2006

Frankl, Viktor Emil. *The Unheard Cry For Meaning.* Touchstone Books, 1979

Freiberg, Kevin and Jackie. *Guts! Companies that Blow the Doors off Business-as-usual.* Currency, 2003

Fritz, Robert. *The Path of Least Resistance.* Butterworth-Heinemann Ltd., 1994

Gerber, Michael, *The E-Myth Revisited: Why Most Small Businesses Don't Work and What to Do About It.* Collins, 1995

Goleman, Daniel. *Emotional Intelligence.* Bloomsbury Publishing PLC, 1996

Gozdz, Kazimierz (ed). *Community Building: Renewing Spirit and Learning in Business.* New Leaders Press, 1996

Hammond, Sue Annis and Andrea B. Mayfield. *The Thin Book of Naming Elephants: How to Surface Undiscussables for Greater Organizational Success.* Thin Book Publishing Co., 2004

Hankins, Gerald W. Rolling *On: The Story of the Amazing Gary McPherson.* The University of Alberta Press, 2003

Isaacs, William. *Dialogue: The Art Of Thinking Together*. Currency, 1999

Johnson, Steven. *Emergence: The Connected Lives of Ants, Brains, Cities, and Software* (reprint). Scribner, 2002

Kao, John. *Jamming*. Harper Collins Canada, 1997

Katzenbach, Jon R. and Douglas K. Smith. *The Wisdom of Teams: Creating the High-Performance Organization* (reprint). Collins Business Essentials, 2003

Kurzweil, Ray. *The Age of Spiritual Machines*. Penguin (Non-Classics), 2000

Kurzweil, Ray. *The Singularity Is Near: When Humans Transcend Biology*. Penguin, 2006

Loeb, Paul Rogat, ed. *The Impossible Will Take a Little While: A Citizen's Guide to Hope in a Time of Fear*. Basic Books, 2004

Meyer, Christopher and Stan Davis. *It's Alive: The Coming Convergence of Information, Biology, and Business*. Crown Business, 2003

Norretranders, Tor. *The User Illusion: Cutting Consciousness Down to Size*. Penguin Press Science, 1999

O'Connor, Joseph and Ian McDermott. *The Art of Systems Thinking: Essential Skills for Creativity and Problem Solving*. Thorsons, 1997

Peters, Tom. *Thriving on Chaos: Handbook for a Management Revolution*. Harper Paperbacks, 1988

Peterson, Christopher. *Journal of Personality and Social Psychology*. University of Michigan, 1989

Pressfield, Steven. *The War of Art: Break Through the Blocks and Win Your Inner Creative Battles*. Warner Books, 2003

Putnam, Robert D. *Bowling Alone: The Collapse and Revival of American Community*. Simon & Schuster, 2001

Scharmer, Otto, et al. *Presence: An Exploration of Profound Change in People, Organizations, and Society*. Currency, 2005

Senge, Peter M. *The Fifth Discipline: The Art & Practice of The Learning Organization*. Currency, 2006

Senge, Peter M., C. Otto Scharmer, Joseph Jaworski and Betty Sue Flowers: *Presence: An Exploration of Profound Change in People, Organizations, and Society*. Currency, 2005

Shaw, Bernard. *Man And Superman: a Comedy And a Philosophy*. Kessinger Publishing, 2005

Siebert, Al. *The Resiliency Advantage: Master Change, Thrive Under Pressure, and Bounce Back from Setbacks*. Berrett-Koehler Publishers, 2005

Turnbull, Colin. *The Forest People*. Touchstone Book, 1987

Wheatley, Margaret J. and Myron Kellner-Rogers. *A Simpler Way*. Berrett-Koehler Publishers, 1998

Whitney, Diana L. and Amanda Trosten-Bloom. *Encyclopaedia of Positive Questions: Using AI to Bring Out the Best in Your Organization (Tools in Appreciative Inquiry)*, Volume I. Lakeshore Communications, 2001

Wilber, Ken. *A Theory of Everything: An Integral Vision for Business, Politics, Science and Spirituality*. Shambhala, 2001

Index

Go Deeper Index

 This is an alphabetical listing of the Go Deeper topics found throughout the text. You can explore these ideas in more depth through the Web site *www.anthillsite.com*. There you will find web links connected to various topics.

Speaking & Consulting

Contact us at:

WWW.CQatWork.com

Toll Free 1 866 912 5210

info@CQatWork.com

Take the CQ Challenge

When has your teams' CQ been at its most obvious? We would love to hear about it.

- What was going on?
- What made it special?
- And what did the team achieve?

The example you send us could be featured in the next edition of *Teaching an Anthill to Fetch*, so send us your CQ stories, we'd love to see them.

In the meantime you could also go to *WWW.CQatWork.com* and take the **CQ Quiz**. Everyone who takes the quiz receives a free report on the ten ways of developing more CQ @ work.

About the Author

Stephen's first presentation was to a large group by anyone's standards; 40,000. However, at the tender age of 12 he realized that chickens are a tough audience. Inspiring them to change their lives was very hard work. He often wonders where those chickens who did listen to him are now.

Stephen comes from a long line of story-tellers. After all, in Ireland it is a national sport. But everything wasn't sweetness and light as he grew up during the "troubles" in early 70s Northern Ireland. The farm he grew up on was situated in the so-called "murder triangle". Political violence was an everyday reality. Although the Irish are bright people, they had very poor collaborative intelligence. This was where Stephen's fascination with what enables people to "get-on" was born.

An accomplished psychotherapist and business consultant Stephen has been consulting for over ten years in health care, non-profit, professional associations, education, and government. He is the founder and principle of Zenergy PD and acts as the resilience content expert for one of Canada's largest health authorities. For over a quarter of a century Stephen has been researching the dynamics of change, problem resolution, group dynamics, and his greatest passion — *collaborative intelligence*. Extensively trained in NLP (neuro-linguistic programming), facilitation, improv, and group dynamic techniques, Stephen engages his audiences with customized "one-off" events that bring each participant deeply into the topic.

Just as important for Stephen, he is a father, husband, and an active participant in his community. He serves on several boards associated with socio-economic development and is a staunch advocate of the triple bottom line as a path towards a sustainable society.

Little Known Facts about Stephen Joyce

At one point in his life he managed to run himself over with his own car. Not a great idea granted, but you must give him some credit for sheer inventiveness.

In 1982, while at Bristol University, Stephen held the UK *Guinness Book of Records* title for the most live earth worms eaten in 60 seconds (long before the days of *Fear Factor*). Stephen claims he did it to raise money for charity and that he had the written permission of every last worm.

When he was a child, Stephen's best friend was a paraplegic pig called Herbie to whom he told all his darkest secrets. Unfortunately Herbie disappeared one day when Stephen was at school and was never seen again. It's a cruel blow to discover you've eaten your best friend.

Stephen lives "outside the box" but drops in occasionally
to collect his mail — stephenjoyce@CQatwork.com